W9-CFB-471

A Practical Guide to Needs Assessment

A Practical Guide *to* Needs Assessment

Kavita Gupta

JOSSEY-BASS/PFEIFFER
A Wiley Company
www.pfeiffer.com

Published by

JOSSEY-BASS/PFEIFFER

A Wiley Company
989 Market Street
San Francisco, CA 94103-1741
415.433.1740; Fax 415.433.0499
800.274.4434; Fax 800.569.0443

www.pfeiffer.com

Jossey-Bass/Pfeiffer is a registered trademark of John Wiley & Sons, Inc.

ISBN: 0-7879-3988-9
Library of Congress Catalog Card Number 98-25370

Library of Congress Cataloging-in-Publication Data

Gupta, Kavita, 1958-
A practical guide to needs assessment / by Kavita Gupta.
p. cm.
"ASTD (American Society for Training and Development)."
Includes bibliographical references and index.
ISBN 0-7879-3988-9
1. Training needs—Evaluation. 2. Needs assessment. I. American
Society for Training and Development. II. Title.
HF5549.5.T7 G87 1999
658.3'124–ddc21   98-25370

Printed in the United States of America

Printing   10   9   8

We at Jossey-Bass strive to use the most environmentally sensitive paper stocks available to
us. Our publications are printed on acid-free recycled stock whenever possible, and our paper
always meets or exceeds minimum GPO and EPA requirements.

Jossey-Bass also publishes its books in a variety of electronic formats. Some content that
appears in print may not be available in electronic books.

Contents

List of Figures

List of Toolkit Forms

Acknowledgments

I WISH TO THANK all the following people who helped in some fashion to pull this book together; either through their advice, feedback, or support:

Chris Morton, Mel Silberman, Michael Molenda, Bruce Griffiths, Betsy Frick, Anne Harrington, Pat Vallely, Anne Durgin, Margaret Driscoll, Linda Barrile, and Kathy Tully.

I am also grateful to those who contributed the cases: Bob Carroll, Anne Marie Dyckman, Mary Keller, and Jeanne Strayer.

And finally I owe my gratitude to friends and family, and the Jossey-Bass/Pfeiffer team, especially Larry Alexander for his patience.

Saint Louis, Missouri   *Kavita Gupta*
August 1998

Introduction

NEEDS ASSESSMENT is an important step in the performance improvement business. It precedes the design and development of any human resource development initiative.

A needs assessment may involve examining performance improvement opportunities for people across job functions. It can also involve identifying and solving performance problems at a group or individual level.

As human resource development (HRD) professionals, we must often work with other business partners to perform needs assessments. We must do this to diagnose performance needs accurately and to provide practical solutions that address the business needs of an organization, but we often lack the knowledge, skills, or tools to conduct an effective assessment or we are confused about which approach to use, given the wide array of choices.

PURPOSE OF THIS BOOK

The purpose of this book is to bridge the gap between theory and practice. Over the years, scores of practitioners have expressed their frustration at the lack of resources that describe needs assessment in layman's terms. Although a number of books exist on the subject, they are either high-level and designed for an elite audience or too complex for those in the trenches who need to do the job.

The objective of this one-stop guide is to provide practitioners with *how-to* answers to fundamental questions, such as: How is a training needs assessment done? What are the steps involved in a competency-based assessment?

AUDIENCE FOR THE BOOK

This book is intended primarily for HRD practitioners in businesses and nonprofit organizations looking for systematic approaches for conducting needs assessments. It is for those practitioners who must validate the introduction of an HRD program. It is also for human performance improvement consultants confronted with client demands for assessing the development needs of the workforce.

The book is useful for HRD professionals from both the public and private sectors worldwide, including training and HR directors or managers, trainers, training or HR generalists, administrators, performance consultants, and HRD consultants.

The book is also appropriate for a secondary audience that consists of small business owners, family-owned businesses, and heads of small- or medium-sized organizations. This includes those who perform needs assessments on an occasional basis.

SCOPE OF THE BOOK

The book lays the foundation for sound needs assessment practice through some initial grounding in the "whats" and "whys" of the process. This is followed by the how-tos of needs assessment. The book includes:

- A framework for understanding needs assessment and the underlying philosophy for doing one,
- A step-by-step approach for launching and implementing a variety of needs assessments,

- A toolkit with forms and worksheets that can be used immediately, provided both in hard copy and on a disk, and

- A glossary to facilitate the use of a common language among HRD practitioners.

Using a straightforward approach, the guide is designed to ensure that you stay on target with your initiative. Its no-frills style also allows you to reach the heart of the subject matter quickly and apply the principles right away.

HOW THE BOOK IS ORGANIZED

Figure I.1 shows how the book is organized. Part One begins with a bird's eye view of needs assessment and provides an overview of basic data-gathering concepts.

Part Two describes four main approaches to needs assessment. The chapters are arranged in sequential order and follow a top-down approach, in that macro approaches, such as strategic needs assessment, are presented first.

Part Two outlines when to use each approach and describes the benefits, drawbacks, and critical success factors of each. Where appropriate, time-saving tips are offered. Key steps are explained, and corresponding forms and worksheets in the Toolkit section are referenced. Case studies follow a standard format and begin with a statement of the need, followed by the approach used and end results achieved.

Part Three includes a variety of templates. These can be replicated and used as they are or customized by making changes on the disk that is included with this book.

A brief summary of each chapter follows:

Chapter One introduces basic concepts related to needs assessment. The scope, methodology, and key features of several needs-assessment

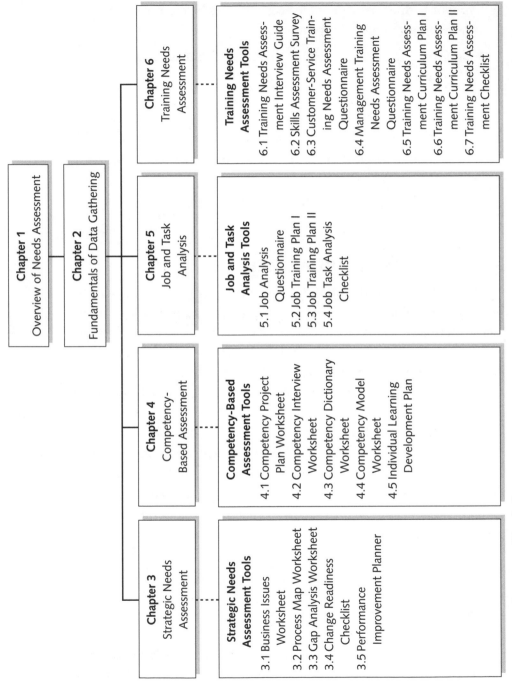

Chapter 1
Overview of Needs Assessment

Chapter 2
Fundamentals of Data Gathering

Chapter 3
Strategic Needs Assessment

Chapter 4
Competency-Based Assessment

Chapter 5
Job and Task Analysis

Chapter 6
Training Needs Assessment

Strategic Needs Assessment Tools

3.1 Business Issues Worksheet
3.2 Process Map Worksheet
3.3 Gap Analysis Worksheet
3.4 Change Readiness Checklist
3.5 Performance Improvement Planner

Competency-Based Assessment Tools

4.1 Competency Project Plan Worksheet
4.2 Competency Interview Worksheet
4.3 Competency Dictionary Worksheet
4.4 Competency Model Worksheet
4.5 Individual Learning Development Plan

Job and Task Analysis Tools

5.1 Job Analysis Questionnaire
5.2 Job Training Plan I
5.3 Job Training Plan II
5.4 Job Task Analysis Checklist

Training Needs Assessment Tools

6.1 Training Needs Assessment Interview Guide
6.2 Skills Assessment Survey
6.3 Customer-Service Training Needs Assessment Questionnaire
6.4 Management Training Needs Assessment Questionnaire
6.5 Training Needs Assessment Curriculum Plan I
6.6 Training Needs Assessment Curriculum Plan II
6.7 Training Needs Assessment Checklist

FIGURE I.1 *Overview of Book Contents*

models are presented. A matrix gives an overview of the needs-assessment approaches described in the book.

Chapter Two presents guidelines for preparing and conducting interviews, focus groups, and observations. Factors to take into consideration when developing surveys and questionnaires are explained, along with tips for communicating results.

Chapter Three is the first in the series of how-to chapters. This chapter shows how to link performance problems and performance needs to the business strategy of an organization. Porter's Five-Force Model for analyzing the external environment is explained, and guidelines for using process maps are also given.

Chapter Four explains how to do a competency-based assessment. The steps for developing competencies using behavioral interviews are presented, and a competency dictionary and competency model are described.

Chapter Five explains how to write effective job and task statements. Steps for performing a job task analysis are given, and how to formulate a training plan after this information has been obtained is also shown.

Chapter Six describes the steps for doing a conventional training needs assessment, along with strategies for conducting a needs assessment.

HOW TO USE THE BOOK

How you use this book depends on two factors: your level of experience and your specific situation. If you are new to the profession or have little prior knowledge about needs assessment, consider reviewing all the chapters first. You can then use the information immediately or assimilate it and use it at a later date. For instance, if you want to conduct a job and task analysis for technicians right away, then consult Chapter Five. You can also use the corresponding Toolkit templates.

At a later date, you may want to perform a competency study for first-line supervisors. The guidelines outlined in Chapter Four, as well as the forms and worksheets, can help provide a head start on this type of assessment.

If you have prior knowledge or experience with needs assessment, skim through the contents of Part One. Then home in on those chapters in Part Two in which more information is given.

This guide is designed to provide you with resources that you can tailor to the needs of your organization. As different assessment opportunities arise in the workplace, consider using one, or a combination, of the techniques that are outlined in this book to proceed with your project. For a quick reference guide to the chapters, see Figure I.2.

To	Consult
Review the book's contents	Introduction
Examine different needs-assessment models	Chapter 1
Obtain an overview of needs-assessment approaches (purpose, when to use, advantages, disadvantages, key tools, and outputs)	Chapter 1
Identify which data-gathering method to employ in a needs assessment	Chapter 2
Link performance problems or performance needs to the business strategy of an organization	Chapters 1, 2, and 3
Develop a long-term performance improvement plan	Chapters 1, 2, and 3
Identify competencies for effective performance Build success profile for people, particularly in supervisory or managerial jobs Assess gaps in proficiency levels and formulate training or performance management systems	Chapters 1, 2, and 4
Identify knowledge, skills, and abilities needed for a specific job or task Develop a job description Develop a job training plan	Chapters 1, 2, and 5
Identify training needs	Chapters 1, 2, and 6

FIGURE I.2 *Quick Reference Guide to Chapters*

TOOLKIT FORMS ON DISK

The disk at the back of this book was designed to be used in conjunction with *A Practical Guide to Needs Assessment.* This disk contains a Microsoft® Word version of the Toolkit forms found in Part Three of this book. The forms may be customized to meet your needs and used for multiple projects. Further information on this disk can be found on p. 210.

I

Putting Things in Context

ONE Overview of Needs Assessment

PURPOSE

This chapter will enable you to accomplish the following:

- Identify the purpose of a needs assessment;
- Define key terms;
- Compare six needs-assessment models in the field; and
- Examine four approaches to needs assessment.

OVERVIEW

Consider the following typical needs statements:

- "Can you give our technicians some training? They are having trouble understanding those Level III manuals."
- "I think my staff needs a time-management training program. They are always late for meetings."
- "Can you develop a three-year performance improvement plan for the company's first-line supervisors?"

To HRD professionals, these statements probably sound familiar. In today's business climate, the need for training has become more pronounced than ever before, but at the same time, organizations have also become cautious about how their training dollars are spent.

Given this situation, it seems obvious that all performance improvement initiatives should begin with a systematic assessment of training needs to ensure that training programs have relevance to the people being trained. Of course, for the past forty years, many researchers and practitioners have said that *some* performance problems can be addressed by training, but not all, so in many cases, non-training interventions are necessary.

In a broad sense, needs assessment can be described as a process for identifying the knowledge and skills necessary for achieving organizational goals (Brinkerhoff & Gill, 1994). It has also been described as a method of finding out the nature and extent of performance problems and how they can be solved (Molenda, Pershing, & Reigeluth, 1996). To understand what needs assessment is all about, let us define a few terms:

- *Gap.* A gap is the difference between what is and what should be—the difference between an actual state (what results are) and a desired state (what results should be) (Kaufman, Rojas, & Mayer, 1993).

- *Needs Assessment.* Needs assessment is a process for pinpointing reasons for gaps in performance or a method for identifying new and future performance needs.

- *Knowledge.* Knowledge is what people need to know, such as subject matter, concepts, or facts, in order to do a job.

- *Skills or Abilities.* Skills (or abilities) are what people must know in order to perform a job.

- *Competencies.* Competencies are the knowledge, skills, attitudes, values, motivations, and beliefs people must have in order to be successful in a job.

NEEDS-ASSESSMENT MODELS

An overview of needs assessment is incomplete without an understanding of the sources from which current methods and practices are drawn. Although many other needs-assessment models exist, only a few are presented here.

The purpose of this section is to introduce you to the work of a few pioneers who made significant inroads to the HRD profession, particularly in the area of needs assessment. These individuals and the models associated with each are listed below and will be described in the upcoming paragraphs:

- Thomas Gilbert: Human Competence Model,
- Joe Harless: Front-End Analysis,
- Roger Kaufman: Organizational Elements Model,
- Robert Mager: Analyzing Performance Problems,
- Allison Rossett: Training Needs Assessment, and
- Geary Rummler: Performance Improvement by Managing the White Space.

A brief synopsis of each model follows. Supplement this introductory information with further reading, using the resource listing provided at the back of the book.

Thomas Gilbert: Human Competence Model

Gilbert is best known for his work on human performance engineering. Gilbert's (1978) basic premise is that human performance is affected by six factors: information, resources, and incentives (the environment), as well as knowledge, capacity, and motives (the individual). As Gilbert says in the book, *Human Competence: Engineering Worthy Performance*, examining these six factors before investing in training can save an organization costly training dollars.

Joe Harless: Front-End Analysis

Harless' earliest work, *An Ounce of Analysis Is Worth a Pound of Objectives*, set the stage for front-end analysis. According to Harless (1970), organizations have an overwhelming tendency to look for answers or solutions when confronted with problems. They tend to do this even before a problem has been defined. Like Gilbert, Harless believes that training is not the solution to all performance problems, but that through front-end analysis, the root cause of performance problems can be uncovered.

More recently, Harless' work has focused on the development of a new performance improvement system: Accomplishment-Based Curriculum Development (ABCD). Using this system, a diagnostic front-end analysis is performed for problems that relate to shortfalls in the current business goals of an organization. A new performance front-end analysis is conducted when organizations have "new performance needs." Harless' model features job aids to guide each step in the process (Ripley, 1997).

Roger Kaufman: Organizational Elements Model

Kaufman's (1996) Organizational Elements Model (OEM) is made up of the following:

- *Inputs.* The resources and ingredients that an organization uses (such as goals or policies),

- *Processes.* The methods, means, procedures, and activities used to achieve desired results,

- *Products.* The building blocks used to achieve desired results,

- *Outputs.* The end results that are delivered outside an organization, and

- *Outcomes.* The effects or payoffs that clients and society realize as a result of the process.

Robert Mager: Analyzing Performance Problems

Mager's contribution to the field spans over thirty years. An established leader in the performance improvement business, Mager designed a performance analysis model or "flow chart" that has had wide usage since its inception in the early 1980s. The basic premise of Mager's model is that performance problems and solutions can be uncovered by asking a systematic set of probing questions. Following are the five main areas for probing in Mager's model (1997):

- Describe the problem;
- Explore fast fixes;
- Check consequences;
- Enhance competence; and
- Develop solutions.

Allison Rossett: Training Needs Assessment

According to Rossett (1987), a gap between an optimal and actual situation results in discrepancies in performance. Using Rossett's purpose-based model, five types of information are gathered during a needs assessment:

- *Optimal Performance or Knowledge.* How performance should be,
- *Actual or Current Performance or Knowledge.* How performance is,
- *Feelings of Trainees and Significant Others.* How people feel about a problem,
- *Causes of the Problem from Many Perspectives.* Reasons for problems, and
- *Solutions to the Problem from Many Perspectives.* Ways to solve a problem.

In the book *Training Needs Assessment* (1987), Rossett describes a six-step process for conducting needs assessment.

Geary Rummler: Performance Improvement by Managing the White Space

Rummler's (1995) basic framework for improving performance is based on an examination of three levels of performance: the organization, processes, and individual jobs or performers. According to Rummler, a holistic approach is necessary in order for performance improvement to occur.

Rummler's model includes five phases and fourteen steps. In the first phase, a performance improvement project is defined. The second phase involves examining performance variables at the organizational level (such as goals). During the third phase, gaps in processes are identified using relationship maps and process maps. Fourth-phase activities are geared toward examining performance improvement opportunities at the job and individual level. In the last phase, performance improvement plans are implemented.

Figure 1.1 summarizes the key features of all the models presented above.

NEEDS-ASSESSMENT APPROACHES

As discussed earlier, this book presents four approaches to needs assessment that have been created to provide a frame of reference—something you can use to grasp new concepts. The classifications have been designed to ensure ease of learning.

Figure 1.2 shows the time and labor needed for any of the approaches. Approaches that fall in the top portion of the chart are more time- and labor-intensive. Figure 1.3 is a summary of when to use each approach. Key tools and outputs for each approach are shown.

Whichever approach you decide to use, take into consideration the political reality of how to do needs assessments in the workplace. First,

	Scope	Methodology	Key Features
Gilbert	Two levels of assessment: work environment and individual	Examine factors in work environment that have an impact on performance first. Then examine individual factors.	• Cube-shaped behavior model • Six cells • $PIP = \dfrac{\text{Exemplary Performance}}{\text{Typical Performance}}$
Harless	Multi-phase performance improvement process	Use rigorous and systematic front-end analysis to improve existing and new human performance in organizations.	• Front-end analysis • An ounce of analysis is worth a pound of objectives • ABCD system • Job aids
Kaufman	Three levels of assessment: mega, macro, and micro	Use five elements of the OEM model to identify what every organization does, produces, and delivers.	• Organizational Elements Model (OEM) • Inputs, processes, products, outputs, outcomes
Mager	Systematic approach to solving performance problems	Use a step-by-step performance analysis model to identify performance problems and find solutions to problems.	• Performance analysis flow chart • Could they do it if their lives depended on it?
Rossett	Systematic study of a problem using data and opinions from many sources	Use a six-step approach to plan a needs assessment.	• Purpose-based assessment • Optimals, actuals, feelings, causes, solutions • Optimal – Actual = Need
Rummler	Three levels of performance: organizational, process, job/individual	Use a 14-step model to diagnose performance improvement opportunities and develop a plan for implementing interventions.	• Improve performance by managing the white space in organizations • Relationship map • Process map

FIGURE 1.1 *Comparison of Needs-Assessment Models*

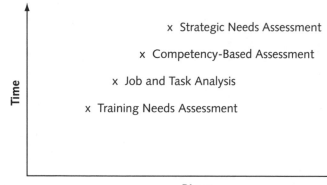

FIGURE 1.2 *Perspective of Needs-Assessment Approaches*

time will always be a critical factor, as most training sponsors will be more concerned about implementing the actual training, as opposed to spending time analyzing needs. Second, most line managers will be reluctant to release personnel to participate in interviews or focus groups, especially if operations will be affected.

Third, you may succeed in finding a champion or sponsor to support your initiative, but face resistance from other groups in the organization that may not perceive the assessment to be as valuable. Finally, in today's fast-paced environment, especially in high-tech industries, training requirements can change so rapidly that data collected during a needs assessment, especially if the assessment spans an extended time frame, can become outdated fairly quickly.

CONCLUSION

The shift from the traditional focus on training and development activities to the performance of individuals and organizations can only come about through a systematic examination of performance needs. This chapter presented an overview of some of the leading practitioners in the field, as well as some of the major needs-assessment approaches.

	Purpose	When To Use	Advantages	Disadvantages	Key Tools	Outputs
Strategic Needs Assessment	Examine existing performance problems (reactive) or address new and future performance needs (proactive) in the context of an organization's business strategy Develop long-term performance improvement plan	Link performance improvement needs to business strategy of organization Identify performance improvement opportunities at organizational, process, and job level	Develop long-term solutions to existing performance problems or new performance needs Solve problems that affect core business processes Eliminate non-value-added activities	Time consuming Costly	Interview Focus group Survey or questionnaire Observation Process map	Performance Improvement Plan

FIGURE 1.3 *Matrix of Needs-Assessment Approaches*

	Purpose	When To Use	Advantages	Disadvantages	Key Tools	Outputs
Competency-Based Assessment	Identify knowledge, skills, and attitudes for superior job performance Build success profile for job function(s)	Identify competencies for managerial, supervisory, or professional jobs Measure proficiency levels of people Develop standardized training Develop performance management systems (recruiting, hiring, promoting, or career planning)	Determine qualities that distinguish average from superior performance Provide information about current and future predictors of job performance Provide accurate and reliable data	Time consuming Requires high involvement of many people within an organization Costly Requires good project management system for large projects	Interview Focus group Survey	Competency Dictionary Competency Model
Job and Task Analysis	Determine responsibilities and tasks necessary to perform a job	Develop new job descriptions or revise existing position profiles	Stimulate interest because people have opportunity to define jobs	Does not take into account external factors that may have impact on job performance	Interview Questionnaire Focus group Observation	Position Profile Job Training Plan

	Purpose	When To Use	Advantages	Disadvantages	Key Tools	Outputs
		Identify task listings for new or redesigned job function(s): knowledge, skills and abilities, and standards Develop consistent training requirements, especially for technical and specialized jobs	Define skill requirements for entry-level versus senior positions Identify additional knowledge, skills, and abilities to move across or upward within a job function Provide accurate and reliable data	Time consuming Costly		
Training Needs Assessment	Identify knowledge and skills to perform a job	Implement new technology Identify training needs Develop training plan	Ensure training is linked to learner's needs Easy to implement	Lacks rigor of strategic needs assessment, competency-based assessment, or job and task analysis	Interview Focus group Survey or questionnaire Observation	Needs Assessment Report Training Plan

FIGURE 1.3 *Matrix of Needs-Assessment Approaches* (continued)

Whether you undertake a strategic approach to needs assessment or perform a competency-based assessment, the message is simple: Needs assessments set the direction for all performance improvement initiatives in an organization, but organizational politics can affect how needs assessments are conducted or implemented in the workplace. Because you are the best judge of what will work in your environment, you can maximize the techniques presented in this book by using those aspects that will result in successful outcomes.

TWO Fundamentals of Data Gathering

PURPOSE

This chapter will enable you to accomplish the following:

- Identify guidelines for preparing and conducting interviews;
- Identify stages for administering focus groups;
- Examine guidelines for preparing and using surveys and questionnaires;
- Recognize tips for performing observations;
- Compare features of interviews, focus groups, questionnaires, and observations;
- Recognize sources of extant data; and
- Identify ways for communicating results.

OVERVIEW

Data gathering is the cornerstone of any needs-assessment project. To identify the training needs of plant personnel, you can conduct a series of interviews. To measure proficiency levels of field engineers, you can conduct a survey. The fundamental premise of needs assessment is that in order to make effective decisions about current or future training needs, data must first be gathered.

There are many ways to collect data. The most commonly used methods are interviews, focus groups, surveys and questionnaires, and observation. Other methods include the nominal group technique, action research, and Dacum (developing a curriculum). It is beyond the scope of this book to discuss these methods. For real-life applications of any of the latter data-gathering techniques, consult the book, *In Action: Conducting Needs Assessment* (Phillips & Holton, 1995).

Usually, data collected from interviews and focus groups can be classified into two categories: qualitative (soft) data and quantitative (hard) data. Qualitative data is difficult to measure because it contains opinions and ideas. Quantitative data can be measured and scored more easily because it is collected using surveys, questionnaires, and observations. Most needs assessments employ one or several data-gathering techniques. The following sections will discuss each of these methods in more detail.

INTERVIEWS

Interviews are one of the easiest tools for gathering information about organizational or performance problems. A brief discussion with customer service associates can help uncover reasons why phone calls are not being handled properly. A more in-depth discussion with senior management can help clarify perspectives on strategic training issues. Interviews can be conducted in two ways: *one-on-one* or *by phone.*

The biggest benefit of one-on-one interviews is the human interaction that occurs. They also allow interviewers to observe facial gestures and pick up nonverbal cues from respondents. Phone interviews are useful when people cannot be accessed easily. They are also beneficial when people do not have the time to meet in person. Phone interviews are more effective when small pieces of information must be gathered. When conducting phone interviews, it is useful to remember the following:

- Use a moderate tone;

- Avoid speaking too rapidly;

- Keep the discussion focused; and

- Probe for responses to your questions.

Both one-on-one and phone interviews can be conducted in either a structured or unstructured manner. In *structured interviews,* a formal set of objectives and a corresponding list of questions is used to guide the interview process. In *unstructured interviews,* questions are not listed in advance. Rather, a list of objectives and topics to be covered during the interview is used.

One-on-one and phone interviews can also be conducted using scripts. In *scripted interviews,* the entire contents of an interview are written out, rehearsed, or practiced in advance. Scripts are useful when multiple interviewers are involved in the data-gathering process. A script combined with an interview protocol ensures that accuracy and consistency of data are maintained. The disadvantage of scripted interviews is that they inhibit spontaneity.

The matrix in Figure 2.1 presents some general guidelines for preparing and conducting interviews. As the figure indicates, the guidelines are similar for most needs-assessment approaches.

FOCUS GROUPS

A focus group is another qualitative data-gathering method. With this group-interview method, people who share similar expertise are brought together and asked their opinions and ideas about a particular topic. Most groups are made up of five to twelve people.

To be effective, focus groups require good facilitators. As Schwarz (1995) points out, facilitators who are conducting focus groups should remember that they are not content experts, mediators, arbitrators, or

17

ring	Strategic Needs Assessment	Competency-Based Assessment	Job and Task Analysis	Training Needs Assessment
ʃamiliarize yourself with technical and industry-specific terms.	✔	✔	✔	✔
. Obtain background information about the problem if possible.	✔		✔	✔
3. Establish interview objectives.	✔			✔
4. Determine whether interviews will be conducted in person or by phone.	✔			✔
5. Identify a comfortable and private location for conducting one-on-one interviews.	✔	✔	✔	✔
6. Limit one-on-one interviews to two hours.	✔		✔	✔
7. Notify managers or supervisors if interviewees will be participating in one-on-one interviews.	✔	✔	✔	✔
8. Send letter of introduction to participants: • State objectives. • Explain why they have been selected. • Specify whether confidentiality will be maintained. • Explain how results will be used. • Specify a time for a follow-up call to make an appointment.	✔	✔	✔	✔
9. Call interviewees to schedule interview: • Allow 20 to 30 minutes between interviews (to document results). • Allow flexibility in scheduling to accommodate those working in shifts.	✔	✔	✔	✔
10. Decide how information will be recorded. Notes? Tape recording?	✔	✔	✔	✔
11. Develop interview protocol if multiple interviewers will be involved.	✔	✔	✔	✔

Note: Boxes that do not contain check marks denote items that are not applicable.

Figure 2.1 *Tips for Preparing and Conducting Interviews*

Developing Questions	Strategic Needs Assessment	Competency- Based Assessment	Job and Task Analysis	Training Needs Assessment
12. Ensure that each question matches a stated objective.	✔			✔
13. Place important questions at the beginning.	✔			✔
14. Place controversial or sensitive questions at the end.	✔			✔
15. Specify the amount of time to be spent on each question.	✔	✔	✔	✔
16. Sequence questions from general to specific.	✔		✔	✔
17. Sequence and cluster questions in a logical order.	✔		✔	✔
18. Ensure that questions are clear, concise, and jargon-free.	✔	✔	✔	✔
19. Be sure that questions are appropriate for the skill level and experience of the target audience.	✔	✔	✔	✔
20. Provide adequate space between questions to record information.	✔	✔	✔	✔
21. Pilot test interview questions.	✔	✔	✔	✔
22. Make appropriate revisions.	✔	✔	✔	✔

Conducting the Interview	Strategic Needs Assessment	Competency- Based Assessment	Job and Task Analysis	Training Needs Assessment
23. Begin with a few rapport-building questions.	✔	✔	✔	✔
24. Obtain permission to record the interview.	✔	✔	✔	✔
25. Avoid maintaining rigidly to question sequence. Be flexible, but ensure that all questions have been covered by the end. If not, schedule a follow-up phone interview.	✔			✔

Note: Boxes that do not contain check marks denote items that are not applicable.

Figure 2.1 *Tips for Preparing and Conducting Interviews (continued)*

Conducting the Interview (continued)	Strategic Needs Assessment	Competency-Based Assessment	Job and Task Analysis	Training Needs Assessment
26. Give all participants an equal amount of time to respond to each question.	✔	✔	✔	✔
27. Clarify responses when necessary.	✔	✔	✔	✔
28. Ask for concrete examples to support statements.	✔	✔	✔	✔
29. Separate facts from opinions.	✔	✔	✔	✔
30. Maintain a neutral attitude.	✔	✔	✔	✔
31. Avoid discussing results with other interviewees.	✔	✔	✔	✔
32. Ask whether interviewees have additional questions at the end.	✔	✔	✔	✔
33. Offer appreciation for participation.	✔	✔	✔	✔
34. Summarize key points.	✔	✔	✔	✔
35. Ask whether interviewees can be contacted again if necessary.	✔	✔	✔	✔

Note: Boxes that do not contain check marks denote items that are not applicable.

Figure 2.1 *Tips for Preparing and Conducting Interviews (continued)*

judges. Schwarz suggests that facilitators should follow these tips when conducting focus groups:

- Accept responses in a nonjudgmental manner;
- Avoid making decisions about a group's work; and
- Encourage an atmosphere of openness and mutual respect.

Administering focus groups involves three stages: *preparing, conducting,* and *reporting.* An overview of the tasks involved in each stage is given below.

Preparing

Preparing for a focus group involves several activities. Facilitators must identify the purpose of the meeting, establish objectives, prepare an agenda, and select the target audience. In addition, they must schedule appointments, prepare and pilot questions, and gather resources for a session.

Conducting

When conducting a session, facilitators must balance several tasks, such as the following:

- Review the facilitator's qualifications and experience;
- Review the agenda and objectives of the session;
- Clarify the facilitator's and participants' roles;
- Clarify ground rules for participation;
- Chart responses on a flip chart;
- Lead and facilitate the discussion; and
- Encourage active participation.

Reporting

The last stage in administering a focus group involves two steps: *summarizing results* and *preparing a report.* For a sample list of items to include in a report, see the section titled "Tips for Communicating Results" at the end of the chapter.

SURVEYS AND QUESTIONNAIRES

Developing good surveys and questionnaires is not easy, but following a systematic process can ensure that objectives and desired end results are achieved. There are several stages involved in preparing and implementing surveys and questionnaires:

- Preparing,
- Designing,

- Developing questions,
- Writing instructions,
- Writing cover letters, and
- Pilot testing.

Each of the above stages is discussed in further detail below.

Preparing

Before constructing a survey or questionnaire, it is useful to familiarize yourself with difficult terms. If necessary, consider using a subject-matter expert to translate technical jargon into simpler language.

You may also want to observe people in their work environments or review reports. Observations can provide useful information about how people perform actual job tasks. Reports can provide figures, indices, or trends that can help you to frame more specific questions. Another critical step during the preparatory stage is to establish a goal for your needs-assessment project.

Designing

When designing a survey or questionnaire, it is important to take the following factors into consideration:

- *The Size of the Survey.* If the group will be large, use closed-ended questions that can be scored and tabulated easily by a computer. (More detail about closed-ended questions is provided below.) If qualitative information is also required as part of the analysis, conduct separate interviews or focus groups to collect this additional data.

- *How Data Will Be Analyzed.* Most electronically scanned instruments can be designed in-house. However, occasionally a survey or questionnaire may require special predesigned bar codes. In such cases, consider using the services of an internal market research department or external agency to provide assistance in instrument design. Often, large universities with data processing departments can also provide this type of service for a nominal fee.

- *Whether Color Schemes Are Used.* Robinson and Robinson (1989) suggest using a color-coding system if a large number of surveys will be sent to different sources. This technique facilitates the data-analysis process by allowing surveys to be pre-sorted and distributed easily.

Developing Questions

Nothing is more frustrating than sending out five hundred surveys to find out later that 60 percent of the respondents misinterpreted a question. For this reason, it is crucial to follow a few basic guidelines when developing questions. Most surveys and questionnaires use two types of questions: *open-ended* and *closed-ended questions.*

Open-Ended Questions

Open-ended questions require respondents to answer in their own words. The purpose of this type of question is to elicit in-depth responses, as opposed to limited responses. When preparing open-ended questions, remember to take the following elements into consideration: *sequence, length,* and *complexity.*

Sequence. The sequence in which questions appear is important. Usually, it is more effective to begin a survey or questionnaire with a few simple and interesting questions. Potentially sensitive questions should always be presented later.

Length. Requests for multiple pieces of information should always be divided into separate questions. For example, the question, "Why do you submit a copy of XYZ report and how do you use it?" asks for two pieces of information. In many cases, respondents will either overlook the second portion of the question entirely or just not answer it. A more effective way to present the same question is to ask, "What is the purpose of XYZ report?" and then "How do you use it?" or "Describe three ways in which you use it."

Complexity. Always frame questions so that they can be answered easily. Avoid asking questions that require extensive calculations. For example, consider the question, "How many sales calls do you make in a year?" To answer this question, respondents must compute an annual figure based on weekly and monthly totals. Instead, the same question can be phrased as follows: "How many sales calls do you make per week?"

Closed-Ended Questions

In contrast to open-ended questions, closed-ended questions allow respondents to choose from defined options. The disadvantage of closed-ended questions is that respondents cannot elaborate on their answers. There are several types of closed-ended questions:

- Multiple choice,
- Forced choice or mutually exclusive questions (yes or no questions), and
- Scales of various kinds.

Multiple Choice. Multiple choice is the most common type of closed-ended question. These questions usually include a list of four or more answers from which respondents must select one answer.

Forced Choice (Yes/No). Forced-choice questions are used when an answer can be either one thing or the other and they are mutually exclusive.

Nominal Scale. Questions that have no prescribed order and are listed arbitrarily use nominal scales. An example is shown on the next page:

Q. Which of the following departments do you work with most closely?
a. Accounting
b. Information Services
c. Human Resources
d. Marketing
e. Operations

Likert Scale. Questions that ask respondents to rank or rate values and attitudes use Likert (1932) scales. When using Likert scales, it is usually best to assign the most positive value at the high end of the scale (Paul & Bracken, 1995). Two examples follow:

1 = strongly disagree
2 = disagree
3 = somewhat agree
4 = agree
5 = strongly agree

1 = very low
2 = low
3 = average
4 = high
5 = very high

Interval Scales. Questions used to collect demographic data use interval scales. These scales are also useful for obtaining information about a range of possibilities. The following is an example of an interval-scale question:

Q. How many loans do you close in a week?
a. Under 25
b. 25–35
c. 36–45
d. 46–55
e. Over 55

Wording Questions

In order for a survey or questionnaire to be effective, questions must be clear and easy to understand. A few rules of thumb to follow when phrasing questions are given below:

- Use simple words;

- Avoid leading questions such as, "Do you feel that offering the management training program will improve your managerial skills?"; and

- Avoid negatively phrased questions such as, "Did you not receive the computer training?"

Following is a summary of when to use each type of question:

TYPE OF QUESTION	WHEN TO USE
Open-Ended	Capture respondents' own words
	Probe for more information
	Seek more information as a follow-up to a closed-ended question
	Seek opinions
	Responses will be varied
Closed-Ended	Obtain quantitative information
Multiple Choice	Obtain one response from a list of choices
Forced Choice	Obtain opposite or mutually exclusive answers
Nominal Scale	Choice of answers have no rank order
	Obtain information about respondents themselves
Likert Scale	Rank or rate values and attitudes
Interval Scale	Obtain demographic data
	Obtain a response that has a range of possibilities

Writing Instructions

The fourth stage in preparing surveys or questionnaires involves writing explicit instructions. When writing instructions, specify how respondents should complete the form. Explain whether respondents should circle items, use check marks, or write comments. State the amount of time that will be required to complete the survey, to whom it should be returned, and by when.

Writing Cover Letters

Another critical step in implementing surveys and questionnaires is preparing cover letters. Cover letters are essential because they explain why a survey is being sent. In addition, they describe how respondents will benefit from a study. To ensure a good response rate, ask a senior staff member or the president of the company to endorse the importance of the study with his or her signature. State whether the information that is gathered will be kept confidential or not.

Pilot Testing

After a questionnaire has been designed, it is usually a good idea to pilot test it. A pilot test can identify problems in construction and/or physical layout and can also answer the following questions:

- Are instructions clear and concise?
- Can respondents understand the questions easily?
- Can respondents answer questions easily?
- Do respondents have enough space to record comments?

The process of pilot testing consists of several steps. If diverse groups will be surveyed, select a few people from each group or subgroup. In a private meeting room, distribute the form and ask respondents to complete it while you are in the room. Observe the group's reactions closely and watch the people's faces for reactions that may indicate confusion or frustration. Ask respondents to express problems as they are completing the form. Later, summarize the results of the pilot test.

After an initial pilot test, make the appropriate changes to the instrument. Conduct a second pilot test with ten to twenty respondents if the group size is over two hundred (Callahan, 1985). Also try tabulating results to see whether there will be any problems with data analysis later. Figure 2.2 summarizes the steps for preparing and implementing surveys.

OBSERVATION

Observation is the fourth method used to collect data during needs assessments. When used systematically, observation can yield meaningful results. Like interview data, observational data can be collected in a structured or unstructured fashion. *Structured* observations have several advantages:

- They reduce the potential for bias;
- They increase the reliability of observations; and
- They provide an accurate way to report data.

As Rossett suggests (1987), use the unstructured method to obtain an initial feel for a situation. Then follow up with a structured observation. One problem that arises with observation is that people often alter their behavior when under the scrutiny of others. To avoid this problem, use unobtrusive techniques. For example, observe people from a place from which you cannot be viewed. You can also reduce anxiety by dressing in attire similar to your respondents' attire.

Following are a few tips for preparing observation forms:

- Make accommodations for recording both qualitative and quantitative data;

1. Familiarize yourself with the background situation. Speak with appropriate sources to define and clarify jargon or technical terms.

2. Define the goal.

3. Determine whether questions from previously developed surveys can be used in their entirety or in part.

4. Determine whether any commercial surveys or questionnaires can be customized.

5. Determine whether confidentiality will be maintained.

6. Determine how results will be analyzed.

7. Consult with an in-house technical specialist if an electronic survey will be used or if computerized analysis will be performed. Determine whether outsourcing will be necessary.

8. Decide whether color schemes should be used.

9. Decide how results will be presented.

10. Ensure that each question has a purpose.

11. Determine which type of question (open or closed-ended) will elicit the best response. Maintain simplicity if the survey will be sent to a large number of people.

12. Arrange questions in a logical sequence from general to specific.

13. Ensure that each question asks for only one piece of information.

14. Avoid leading and biased questions.

15. Avoid negatively phrased questions.

16. Avoid personal or identifying questions.

17. Ask questions that the respondents are qualified to answer.

18. Avoid jargon, abbreviations, or colloquialisms.

19. Use gender-neutral terms.

20. Write questions that are clear and concise.

21. Position difficult or sensitive questions at the end.

22. Number items.

23. Provide space for comments.

Figure 2.2 *Tips for Preparing and Implementing Surveys and Questionnaires*

24. Limit the use of commas.

25. Use boldface or italic type and underline where appropriate.

26. Use plenty of white space.

27. Number pages.

28. Write instructions on how to answer questions.

29. Explain complicated or confusing terms.

30. Write a cover letter:

- State the purpose of the survey.
- Provide a history of previous research or findings if appropriate.
- Show the benefit to the user.
- Explain why the respondent was selected.
- State when and how the form should be returned.
- Thank the respondent for completing the survey.

31. Pilot test the questionnaire or instrument after it has been developed.

32. Make appropriate modifications based on results of the pilot test.

33. Conduct a second pilot test if necessary.

34. Make final modifications.

35. Use quality paper for copies.

Figure 2.2 *Tips for Preparing and Implementing Surveys and Questionnaires* (continued)

- Do not restrict your form to a series of blank tables, but do provide space for comments and additional notes; and

- Include a checklist of items to be observed: individual tasks and subtasks performed, frequency of performance, or amount of time taken to perform a task with a start and end time.

Figure 2.3 presents a summary of the four primary data-gathering methods discussed above.

Method	When To Use	Time Required		Cost	Resources Required	
		Conduct or Implement	**Analyze Data**		**HRD**	**Management**
One-on-One Interviews	Conduct strategic, competency, job task analysis or training needs assessment Obtain sensitive information Discuss complex issues that require explanations Gain support	High	High	Medium to high	Time Skilled interviewer	Budget Time
Phone Interviews	Conduct strategic or training needs assessment Gather small pieces of information Ask follow-up questions Obtain information when respondents are geographically disbursed	Low to medium	Medium	Low	Time Skilled interviewer	Time

FIGURE 2.3 *Comparison of Primary Data-Gathering Methods*

Method	When To Use	Time Required		Cost	Resources Required	
		Conduct or Implement	Analyze Data		HRD	Management
	Obtain information from many sources quickly Obtain non-sensitive information Obtain more quantifiable and qualitative information Save cost					
Focus Groups	Conduct strategic, competency, job task analysis, or training needs assessment Collect qualitative data Gather information when group behavior determines job performance	Low	High	Medium to high	Time Skilled facilitator Note taker or recorder	Budget Time
Surveys and Questionnaires	Conduct strategic, competency, job task analysis, or training needs assessment Individuals are geographically disbursed	Low to medium	Low	Low	Time Knowledge of survey development	Budget Administrative support

Method	When To Use	Time Required		Cost	Resources Required	
		Conduct or Implement	Analyze Data		HRD	Management
	Obtain quantifiable data Responses to questions can be predicted easily				Data analysis source Data tracking source	
Observations	Conduct strategic, job task analysis, or training needs assessment Document performance Observe frequency of performance Document amount of time taken to perform a task	Low	Low to medium	Low	Time Availability of individuals Knowledge of the performance to be observed Observation form	

FIGURE 2.3 *Comparison of Primary Data-Gathering Methods* (continued)

EXTANT DATA

Another vital source of information in needs assessments is extant data, which can be obtained from many sources, such as business plans, mission statements, job descriptions, performance reviews, training evaluation forms, sales records, customer-service calls, personnel records, and budgets. As these sources indicate, extant data can be qualitative or quantitative. Usually, this method of data collection is optimized when it is used in conjunction with another primary data-gathering method.

The following are a few tips for using extant data:

- Be clear about the type of information you are seeking before undertaking an extensive search of company records;

- Seek permission prior to using archival or company records; and

- Look for trends and patterns in data.

TIPS FOR COMMUNICATING RESULTS

Results from needs assessments vary. During the course of a needs assessment, you may prepare interim as well as final reports. How findings are presented depends largely on the culture of your organization. For some sponsors, a brief executive summary may be adequate. Others may require more in-depth reports.

As a rule of thumb, share findings from a needs assessment with your sponsor on a regular basis. Avoid waiting until the end to report any controversial or unpleasant findings. Seek your sponsor's advice about how to position proprietary findings. Following is a suggested list of items to include in a formal report:

- Executive summary,

- Objectives,

- Methodology,

- Findings,

- Conclusion,

- Recommendations, and

- Appendix (including supporting instruments and data).

In addition, when preparing reports, use pie charts, graphs, diagrams, or histograms to highlight key findings.

CONCLUSION

Data collection and analysis are essential parts of needs assessments. This chapter presented four of the most commonly used methods of data gathering. As seen, each method has its strengths and weaknesses. Needs assessments are optimized when a combination of data-gathering methods is used.

The tools and concepts that were presented in this chapter will be used throughout the book. In addition, you will also learn how to use other tools, such as process maps. The next chapter shows how to use this technique when conducting a strategic needs assessment.

II

Getting Down to Brass Tacks

THREE Strategic Needs Assessment

PURPOSE

This chapter will enable you to accomplish the following:

- Identify the purpose of a strategic needs assessment;

- Recognize when to use the approach;

- Identify the benefits and drawbacks of the approach;

- Recognize critical success factors for performing a strategic needs assessment;

- Identify five phases for conducting a strategic needs assessment; and

- Examine how a strategic needs assessment was performed at a fictitious Company XYZ.

RELATED TOOLKIT JOB AIDS

The following job aids that accompany material in this chapter are available in the Toolkit section of this book:

- Business Issues Worksheet,

- Process Map Worksheet,

- Gap Analysis Worksheet,
- Change Readiness Checklist, and
- Performance Improvement Planner.

OVERVIEW

Every organization faces a variety of performance problems during the course of its business cycle. The scope and magnitude of these performance problems vary. But when the problems affect core business processes, using quick-fix solutions to close performance gaps can be harmful. In such situations, long-term interventions are necessary.

For other organizations, it pays dividends to identify performance needs proactively and develop long-term performance improvement plans that address these needs. This also applies to those in industries undergoing rapid transformations, such as the computer and software industries, banking services, defense operations, or health-care industries.

As Dixit and Nalebuff (1991) explain, to survive chaos, strategic thinking is necessary. As Porter suggests, to sustain competitive advantage, activities should be tailored to the strategy of an organization (1996). A strategic needs assessment provides HRD professionals with a systematic approach for examining existing performance problems or developing solutions to new performance needs. It is focused on identifying internal and external factors that affect performance in the context of the business strategy of an organization.

Before undertaking a strategic performance improvement initiative, it is essential to examine performance gaps in the context in which a business operates. Only then can appropriate solutions be prescribed and a road map for closing the gaps be followed.

Phases III and IV of this chapter provide some guidelines on how to document and identify performance gaps when conducting a strategic assessment. To gain maximum use from a strategic assessment, undertake an initiative of this nature with the help of an internal or external management information systems specialist.

WHEN TO USE

A strategic needs assessment is most effective in the following situations:

- If performance improvement needs must be linked to the business strategy of an organization,

- If performance improvement opportunities must be identified at the organizational, process, and job level,

- If an organization must undertake long-term performance improvement measures, or

- If processes that do not add value to an organization must be identified.

BENEFITS AND DRAWBACKS

Doing a strategic needs assessment has several *benefits*. It allows an organization to do the following:

- Develop long-term solutions to existing performance problems or new performance needs; and

- Solve problems that affect core business processes, such as product development, order processing, or service delivery.

There are two main *drawbacks* to the approach:

- It can be a time-intensive process; and

- It is costly.

CRITICAL SUCCESS FACTORS

The success of a project depends on several factors:

- Sponsorship from executive management,

- Proactive participation of senior management and line management,

- Access to resources such as customers, suppliers, and business resources, and

- Organizational readiness to change.

Before we examine the steps for doing a strategic needs assessment, let us review a few terms that will be used in the chapter.

- *Mission.* A broad statement describing an organization's future plans and directions (see the example in Figure 3.2);

- *Business Goal.* A statement describing a measure or target that will be achieved during a certain period, for example: Become a $100 billion company by the year 2000;

- *Business Unit.* A department or function within an organization, for example, production or operations;

- *Business Process.* A series of activities that provides products, delivers services, or manages resources, for example, accounts receivable within the finance business unit;

- *Process Map.* A graphical illustration of the steps or activities that are performed in a business process (see the example in Figure 3.3 later in this chapter);

- *Process Boundary.* An arbitrary "line" that shows where a business process begins and where it ends, for example, the process boundary for an order management process begins when the customer-service unit sends a mail order and ends when a product is received by a customer; and

- *Performance Improvement Planner.* A blueprint that documents all the performance improvement projects that must be undertaken to improve the overall effectiveness of an organization (see Figure 3.8).

KEY PHASES

A strategic needs assessment is made up of five phases:

Phase I: Assess Current Situation

Phase II: Examine External Environment

Phase III: Examine Internal Environment

1. Validate Business Strategy
2. Document Current Performance
3. Identify Causes of Performance Gaps

Phase IV: Chart Future Environment

Phase V: Develop Performance Improvement Plan

1. Assess Readiness for Change
2. Select Interventions

Each phase is explained below, and the steps within each are given.

Phase I: Assess Current Situation

The purpose of the assessment phase is to develop a better understanding of an existing performance problem. For example, a 30 percent increase in customer complaints would indicate that a problem existed. A mandate from senior management stating that a company's workforce must be prepared for the demands of the 21st Century would indicate a new performance need.

During this phase, it is not necessary to seek information from too many people. Usually, discussions with a few key people can provide enough data to establish preliminary boundaries and a definition of a problem or need. A good starting point is to conduct interviews with a few senior executives from an affected business unit. Later, the span of inquiry can be widened to include middle management and first-line supervisors. See Toolkit Form 3.1 for an interview worksheet that can be used.

In addition, you can also obtain supporting information from secondary sources, such as transcripts of conversations with customers. After you have completed a preliminary analysis, document your findings in a report that includes the following:

- The background of the problem or need,
- The scope of the problem or need,
- The performance improvement goals, and
- The evidence examined.

Phase II: Examine External Environment

Many external factors have an impact on the performance of an organization. After you have developed a better understanding of the problem or need, the next step is to examine these external factors. The purpose of this phase is to:

- Identify and isolate external factors affecting a performance problem or performance need, and
- Determine the implications of these external factors.

Porter's (1980) five-force model offers a useful framework for performing this type of analysis. According to Porter's model, organizations are affected by five factors:

- New competitors who can erode an organization's profitability or market share through cost-cutting measures,

- Major suppliers or supply chains that can raise costs or control the availability of products,

- Substitute products or services that can cause demand for a product to fall,

- Customers who can switch to other products, thus causing profits to drop, and

- Competition among industry players.

A full-fledged five-force analysis is beyond the scope of this book but, as Figure 3.1 shows, the framework serves as a useful tool for determining the threats and opportunities that can impede or enhance the performance of an organization. It also helps to identify the critical business issues that must be taken into consideration when eventually developing a solution.

For example, new and potential entrants, diversification of the computer industry, and entry of suppliers (as shown in the top box of Figure 3.1), can serve as potential threats to a company in the consumer electronics industry. Similarly, price wars, as shown in the box titled "Customers' Power," can result in loss of customers.

Usually, most information pertaining to the external factors affecting a problem or need (the five forces) can be obtained from discussions with the senior leadership of a company. In addition, the following existing sources can be used:

- Industry reports,

- Industry conference proceedings,

- Business newspapers, such as the *Wall Street Journal,*

- Dow Jones Industrial Index,

- Specialized trade journals,

- Market research data,

- Customer-satisfaction surveys,

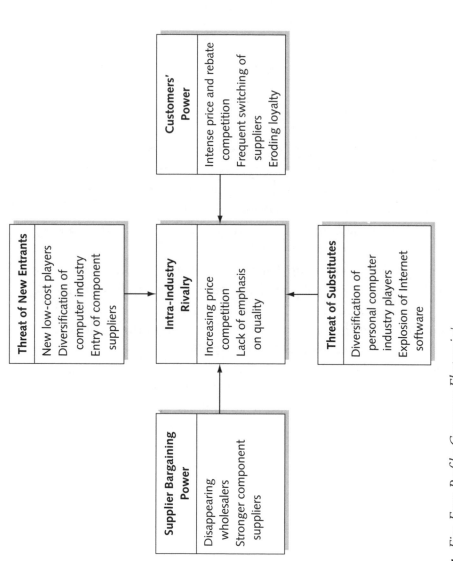

FIGURE 3.1 *Five-Force Profile: Consumer Electronics*[1]

[1]Adapted with the permission of The Free Press, a Division of Simon & Schuster, from *COMPETITIVE STRATEGY: Techniques for Analyzing Industries and Competitors* by Michael E. Porter. Copyright © 1980 by The Free Press.

- Minutes from meetings with customers or suppliers, and

- In-house sales or purchasing databases.

When using the model, it is also helpful to remember that other forces, such as governmental and regulatory restrictions, have an impact on a performance problem or performance need. For instance, a new regulatory bill can cause a slowdown in customer purchases, which in turn can result in lower profits. As Porter (1980) suggests, these additional factors should be examined in the context of the five main factors listed earlier (new competitors, increased costs, available substitutes, eroding customer base, or increased competition).

Phase III: Examine Internal Environment

Phase III provides answers to these questions: What is the organization's competitive strategy given its external environment? Which business processes are affected by the performance problem or performance need? and What are the performance gaps? Depending on the scope of the problem, this phase can take a few days or several months to complete. The steps in this phase: validate business strategy, document current performance, and identify causes of performance gaps are explained below.

Validate Business Strategy

Business strategies are the sets of policies and plans an organization uses to achieve its business goals. They can be found in the business plan of an organization. Figure 3.2 shows an outline of a sample business plan.

An organization's business strategy sets the direction for a performance improvement initiative. It is essential to have this information so that goals for each hierarchical level can be verified and documented.

As Gephart and Van Buren (1996) point out, organizational goals and unit goals across levels, units, and processes should always be aligned. Problems arise only when there is misalignment. The same principles are also emphasized by Rummler (1995) in the book *Improving Performance*.

Mission

Become the most powerful and service-oriented retail company.

Become the leader in every global market served by the end of the decade.

Business Goal

Gain 10 percent of market share by the end of the fiscal year and 20 percent of market share by the end of the second fiscal year.

Introduce three new lines of consumer products by the end of this fiscal year.

Reduce cost of manufacturing top three products by 30 percent.

Other components of a business plan:

- Critical success factors,
- Market analysis,
- Competitive analysis,
- Tactical analysis,
- Financial analysis,
- Head count plan, and
- Profit and loss statement.

FIGURE 3.2 *Sample Business Plan*

Because business plans can be fairly detailed (some can be up to twenty pages long), focus on the strategies and specific tactics that pertain to your particular problem or need. For example, if you are seeking to find out reasons for declining sales, then examine the section that contains marketing business goals. If a business plan is not available or if the information is dated, then conduct interviews or hold a work session with senior executives to obtain this data.

Document Current Performance

After you have confirmed the business strategy, the next step is to examine activities at the process level. By documenting how business process activities are being carried out, potential deficiencies and discrepancies in a process can be identified.

An organization is composed of hundreds of processes and sub-processes. At the highest level, a business process is comprised of seven to fifteen key process steps. One easy way to document the inputs, outputs, and work flows for a business process (or the big picture) is to use *process maps.* Following are a few guidelines, tips, and sample questions to ask a business process owner or supervisor when creating a process map.

As the tips presented on the first page of Toolkit Form 3.2 indicate, remember to maintain perspective about how much detail is necessary when mapping a business process. As Hammer and Champy (1993) suggest, it is critical that processes be kept simple in order to maintain quality, flexibility, and low costs.

An example of a completed process map showing the major activities involved from the time a customer inquiry is received by a bank's Payoff Department until the payoff process is completed is shown in Figure 3.3, a sample of Toolkit Form 3.2.

Figure 3.4 shows sample performance measures that can be used to document business process activities during this stage of the analysis. As the figure shows, the quality of services provided by an accounting unit can be measured by the number of errors processed per bill. In the same way, customer satisfaction can be measured by the number of products returned per thousand units sold. Any deviation from a stated objective(s) is an indication that a problem exists.

Identify Causes of Performance Gaps

There are many reasons for performance gaps. One major cause is activities that do not contribute to business or customer needs. Non-value-added activities result in waste and increase costs. These types of activities must be understood and documented so that gaps in performance can be minimized.

Simple real-life examples of non-value-added activities include unnecessary duplication of tasks, idle or waiting time when no task is being performed, and checking, logging, or approving tasks that were performed correctly. Figure 3.5 shows a more streamlined customer-service process for a fictitious wholesale manufacturer of electronic equipment.

TOOLKIT FORM 3.2 *Process Map Worksheet*

A process map shows the steps or activities that are being performed in a business process. A process boundary shows where a business process begins and ends. For example, the process boundary for order management begins when a customer-service unit sends a mail order and ends when a product is received by a customer.

Instructions

1. To show information received from a source OUTSIDE a process boundary such as a customer, customer request, or another business unit, use a RECTANGLE.

2. To show any activity that is being carried out WITHIN a process such as completing a form, use a CIRCLE.

3. To show the FLOW between activities (INPUTS and OUTPUTS), use an ARROW.

Tips for Process Mapping

1. Document steps in sequence. Try to restrict your diagram to major steps at first. Do not become bogged down in too much detail.

2. Begin by identifying the first major process activity, such as processing quotes, as shown in the figure. Determine the flow of information to and from this process. Use single-pointed arrows for information that flows in one direction. For information that flows between two units or processes, use two-pointed arrows.

3. Identify the next major process. Document the inputs and outputs to this process.

4. Link all major processes as well as inputs and outputs.

   If you cannot define intermediate steps, make notes. Come back to this step later.

5. When you have finished creating your process map, retrace steps to verify accuracy of information collected.

FIGURE 3.3 *Sample Toolkit Form 3.2: Process Map Worksheet*

TOOLKIT FORM 3.2 *Process Map Worksheet*
(continued)

Process: _____

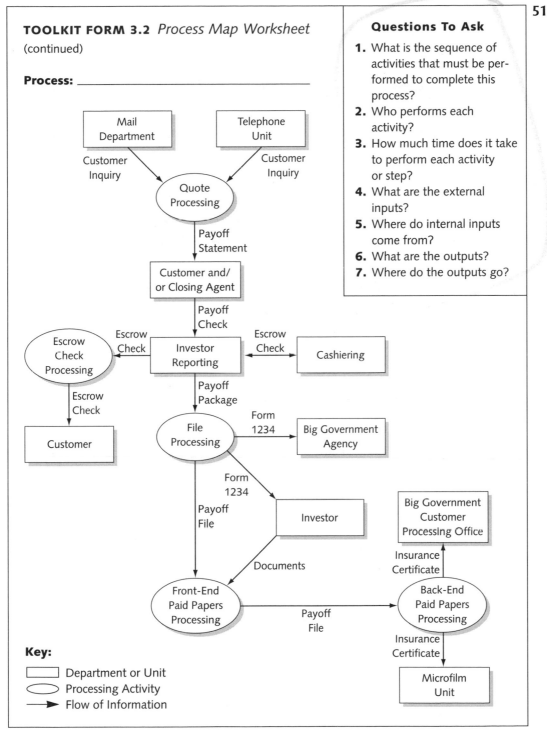

FIGURE 3.3 *Sample Toolkit Form 3.2: Process Map Worksheet* (continued)

Process	Cost	Quality	Time	Customer Satisfaction
Accounting/ Billing	Bills processed per person	Number of errors processed per bill	Amount of time taken to process a bill	Number of bills generated incorrectly
Treasury/ Accounts Receivable	Bank reconciliation per person	Percentage of receivables outstanding past 90 days	Average number of days sales outstanding	Number of posting errors
Production	Average cost per unit below ten cents	Number of defects produced per billion	Amount of orders shipped on time	Number of returns per thousand units sold

FIGURE 3.4 *Sample Performance Measures*

Before Process Improvement

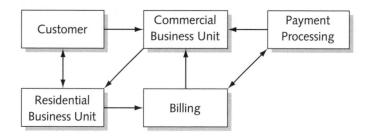

After Process Improvement

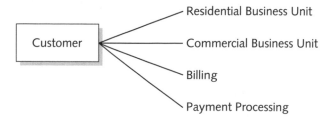

FIGURE 3.5 *Process Map: Company X*

As the figure shows, at first customers who placed calls to the company's service center were transferred to multiple units, but after the process had been streamlined, customer calls were directed to the appropriate area or unit in a more organized manner, resulting in higher levels of efficiency and customer satisfaction. It must be noted that this process of streamlining cannot be done single-handedly. As mentioned earlier, it usually requires the involvement of someone with expertise in management information systems.

Process maps are one method for identifying where performance gaps exist. Other techniques, such as root cause analysis, brainstorming, or problem solving, can also be used to uncover the real cause of problems. To document Phase III activities, use Toolkit Form 3.3. (Also see Figure 3.6, which is a sample of the form.)

Phase IV: Chart Future Environment

After deficiencies and causes of performance gaps have been identified, start creating a map of the desired environment. If you are considering

Process	Current Performance Indicators	Gap	Effect
Quote processing	5 business days	Quotes recorded incorrectly by customer service representatives	Processing delay
Escrow check processing	7 business days	Tax data not received on time	Processing delay
File processing	10 business days	Payoff package incomplete	Processing delay

FIGURE 3.6 *Sample Toolkit Form 3.3: Gap Analysis Worksheet*

a new order-handling or supply-chain management process, then industry leaders such as L. L. Bean, Home Depot, or General Electric can be used as benchmarks.

Usually, the map that is created in this phase is a reconfigured process map at the same level of detail as the one that was created in the previous phase. The main difference is that this map also shows new work flows. Usually, new organizational charts, job classifications, performance measures, or team structures may be necessary to support a new system. By minimizing unnecessary specialization or rigidity in job content, performance at the organizational, process, and job level can be improved. To find guidelines for performing an analysis at the job and task level, see Chapter Five.

Phase V: Develop Performance Improvement Plan

This phase essentially transforms what was mapped in the earlier phase into something more tangible by creating a performance improvement plan or blueprint that documents all the performance improvement projects that must be undertaken to improve the overall effectiveness of an organization. This phase involves two steps, discussed below.

Assess Readiness for Change

First, it is essential to assess whether an organization and its people are ready to implement a performance improvement plan. A formal change readiness plan is particularly necessary when the performance improvement plan will result in significant changes to processes, systems, or jobs. For example, the implementation of a new call-management system may result in the need for a new communications, training, and performance management system.

By making preparations for change, you are building trust among people who will be affected by the change. An open work climate also minimizes people's resistance to change. When launching a change initiative, it is usually best to assign the task to a project leader or facilitator who can manage the whole initiative. See Toolkit Form 3.4 for a checklist that can be used to guide this effort.

Select Interventions

Next, it is necessary to select the interventions that will be most effective for supporting the implementation of an overall performance improvement plan. A performance improvement planner is a useful tool for undertaking this task. Toolkit Form 3.5 shows the factors that must be taken into consideration, such as critical success factors, prerequisites for starting a project, and other related project requirements. Using this systematic approach allows the value and cost of each performance improvement project to be assessed quickly and easily.

The preceding sections presented the methods and tools for doing a strategic needs assessment. Now let us examine how it was done at XYZ Corporation.

CASE STUDY AND TOOLS

This fictitious case shows how Andre Adams, a training director at XYZ Corporation, used a strategic needs assessment approach to develop a long-term performance improvement plan for the company.

This case was contributed by Bob Carroll, an organizational consultant. Carroll has been involved in several performance improvement initiatives for a major computer and health insurance company. The key tools shown here are a Business Issues Worksheet and a Performance Improvement Planner. Highlights of the case are presented below.

XYZ Corporation is a large wholesale distributor of electronics goods. With over $3 billion in assets, the company markets a variety of products to Far Eastern countries, including computers, television and video equipment, and cameras.

The Need

The electronics division of XYZ had not been keeping pace with its other store divisions or with its competition. Sales targets had not been met for two years. The division had been, and could again be, a very lucrative operation for the store. Management wanted to find out what was causing a drop in sales and what actions, if any, were needed to turn things around.

The Approach

The training director used a five-phase approach to conduct the strategic needs assessment. Following is a summary of the phases:

Phase I: Assess Current Situation

1. The training director conducted a series of interviews with the president, two senior vice presidents, and a representative sampling of middle managers and first-line supervisors of the electronics division (see Figure 3.7 for a partially completed summary of these discussions).

2. The training director reviewed one hundred customer-satisfaction surveys taken during the period just before sales began to drop off, then reviewed another one hundred surveys taken during the period when sales went into decline.

3. The training director established preliminary performance improvement goals and prepared a report that summarized the key findings from the first two steps.

Phase II: Examine External Environment

1. The training director conducted research into the business environment in which XYZ and its competitors operated. This was background for a more detailed examination of the consumer electronics market. He consulted industry and trade journals and reviewed customer-satisfaction surveys.

2. He also conducted focus groups with a sample of the division's customers. As a result, the training director discovered that a new Asian competitor was offering lower prices and longer credit periods to customers.

Key business issues	Reduce order delivery time
	Develop new order-management system
	Improve linkage between shipping, receiving, and product delivery
	Improve quality of service to customers
	Improve supplier relationships
	Create ownership in order delivery process
Length problems existed	2 years
Consequences of not solving problems	Lose customers
Business processes affected	Shipping, sales, purchasing
Performance improvement goals	Reduce order delivery time by 50 percent
Obstacles to success	Inability of suppliers to ship goods from overseas on time
	Union rules
	Limit on number of hours shipping and receiving personnel will work on the job

FIGURE 3.7 *Business Issues: XYZ Corporation*

Phase III: Examine Internal Environment

1. The business plan was reviewed for applicability to the changing environment. The business plan revealed that the division was emphasizing quality and speed of delivery instead of lower prices. This was being done despite the fact that the new competitor's low price was hurting sales.

2. Process maps for shipping and purchasing were created and performance gaps identified.

Phase IV: Chart Future Environment

1. The senior leadership of the company and the training director drew up plans for what would be needed to regain lost market share. It was decided that the division would further emphasize its quality and speed by reducing delivery defects and the amount of time taken to produce the goods. Also, greater emphasis would be placed on customer relationships.

2. A reorganization of the shipping and purchasing departments was included in the new plan. It also called for an improved relationship with wholesalers and distributors.

Phase V: Develop Performance Improvement Plan

1. To ensure that the plan would be implemented smoothly, the training director first assessed the organization's readiness for change.

2. Based on the analysis, the following major performance improvement projects were identified:

   • Reduction in order delivery time,

   • Implementation of a new order-management system, and

   • Training to support the implementation of the new order-management system, including team building, relationship management, and customer-service training.

Figure 3.8 shows the performance improvement planner that was used for this project.

The Results

The new order-management system was implemented one year later. Its implementation helped to boost the electronic division's sales. XYZ Corporation regained the market share it had lost. A follow-up survey showed that customer-satisfaction levels were up again.

Project Identification Number: 123

Project Description: Order Delivery Performance Improvement

Project Sponsor (Name/Business Unit): Chuck Brady/Sales

Performance Improvement Goal: Reduce order delivery time from 20 days to 10 days.

Critical Success Factors:

1. Participation of purchasing, shipping, and sales units.

2. Communication of program benefits to customers and employees.

3. Pilot program in two regions before nationwide rollout.

Obstacles to Success:

1. Current shipment vendor's performance.

2. Union rules regarding receiving/shipping job content.

3. Aging inventory computer system.

4. Lack of performance measures for purchasing and shipping supervisors.

Prerequisites for Starting the Project:

1. Improved understanding of customer needs.

2. Vendor participation in sales planning.

Project Structure: Steering committee comprised of unit heads from purchasing, shipping, and sales, project manager, and one analyst from each business unit who understands processes.

Team Requirements: Knowledge of policies in unit, two years' experience in purchasing, shipping, and sales process, operating knowledge of computer system.

Resources: Budget, staff

Expected Cost: $1.2M

FIGURE 3.8 *Performance Improvement Planner: XYZ Corporation*

Benefits:

1. Improved sales - $2.0M

2. Reduced returns - $1.0M

3. Reduced inventory - $2.0M

Timeline

Milestone	Expected Start Date	Expected Completion Date
1. Analysis	1/1	2/28
2. Cost/benefit analysis	3/1	3/5
3. Plan pilot	3/6	3/15
4. Perform pilot	3/16	3/31
5. Launch program	4/1	4/15
6. Rollout program	4/16	4/30

Completed By: _____   Approved By: _____

Date: _____   Date: _____

FIGURE 3.8 *Performance Improvement Planner: XYZ Corporation* (continued)

CONCLUSION

A strategic needs assessment helps solve problems or address needs that are linked to the core business strategies of an organization. It should be used when problems or needs affect core business processes and require long-term interventions.

The success of a performance improvement initiative depends on several factors, including an assessment of an organization's readiness to change and a carefully crafted performance improvement plan. This chapter gave some information on how to extend beyond conventional thinking about needs assessment by examining factors in the external environment that can affect an organization's performance. The focus was on the organization, processes, and jobs. The next chapter will show how to use people and competencies as the basis for performance improvement.

FOUR Competency-Based Assessment

PURPOSE

This chapter will enable you to accomplish the following:

- Determine the purpose of a competency-based assessment;
- Decide when to use the approach;
- Identify the benefits and drawbacks of the approach;
- Recognize critical success factors for performing a competency analysis;
- Explain key terms, such as competency dictionary, core cluster, competency model, and individual learning development plan;
- Identify five phases for conducting a competency-based assessment; and
- Examine how an actual competency analysis was performed at Midsize Community Savings Bank.

RELATED TOOLKIT JOB AIDS

The following job aids for use with the material in this chapter are available in the Toolkit:

- Competency Project Plan Worksheet,
- Competency Interview Worksheet,
- Competency Dictionary Worksheet,
- Competency Model Worksheet, and
- Individual Learning Development Plan.

OVERVIEW

As a professional, you must be able to communicate with and interact effectively with peers, supervisors, and internal or external customers. As a manager, you must be able to lead, solve problems, and act decisively. As a front-line supervisor, you must be able to assume ownership of customer-service problems. These traits are called competencies, which are the enduring characteristics of a person that result in superior on-the-job performance (Spencer, 1995).

Competencies were first introduced in the late 1950s by psychologists Robert White and David McClelland (Dubois, 1993). As McLagan says, "Without clear competency criteria, recruiters select, managers manage, trainers train, and career planners plan to different (and sometimes even conflicting) images of the capabilities required to do a job" (1980, p. 23).

The purpose of a competency-based assessment is two-fold:

- To identify the competencies necessary for superior job performance, and
- To create a composite picture or best-practice model of the competencies necessary for a particular job function or functions.

In a competency-based approach, the focal point is the person or the performer. A competency analysis seeks to identify the knowledge, skills, attitudes, and behaviors needed by a person to excel in a job.

The time taken to complete a competency study varies. Although some studies take a few months to complete, others take several years. The amount of time needed depends on the scope and level of complexity of a project.

WHEN TO USE

A competency approach is most effective:

- When competencies for management, supervisory, or professional jobs must be identified, and

- When a credible system or "template" for recruiting, hiring, developing, and promoting must be developed (Boyatzis, 1982).

BENEFITS AND DRAWBACKS

Doing a competency-based assessment has several *benefits:*

- It establishes the qualities or characteristics that distinguish average from exemplary performance;

- It provides in-depth information about current as well as future predictors of job performance, which helps increase job satisfaction because people have a clear vision about what is expected of them; and

- It can be used to create standardized training and development programs.

Following are a few *limitations* of the approach:

- It is time-consuming because it requires the involvement of many people within an organization, including managers and senior managers, and occasionally may also require the involvement of external agencies such as regulators and customers;

- It is costly to implement; and

- It requires good project management skills.

CRITICAL SUCCESS FACTORS

Several factors are essential to the success of a project (Griffiths, 1997):

- Competencies must produce outcomes that are consistent with the business needs of an organization;

- There must be a sponsor or driver who can leverage a project;

- There must be user ownership, that is, people must be shown what is in it for them in order for a program to be successful;

- The model must be simple enough that people can access and use it easily; and

- The model must be flexible so that it can complement existing performance management systems within an organization.

Before outlining the steps for doing a competency-based assessment, let us review a few terms that will be used in this chapter.

- *Competency Dictionary.* Definition of individual competencies, for example, "projecting": Evaluates current and future market conditions and uses this information to develop sales projections and goals;

- *Core Cluster.* Competencies grouped together under a broad dimension, for example, leadership dimension with core competencies of delegation, coaching, and team building;

- *Competency Model.* A composite picture of the competencies necessary for people to be successful in a job function(s), for example, Toolkit Form 4.4; and

- *Individual Learning Development Plan.* An individual plan that shows the learning activities, support and resources, success indicators, and measures for improving performance, for example, Toolkit Form 4.5.

KEY PHASES

A competency assessment is made up of the following five phases:

Phase I: Develop a Project Plan

1. Establish Parameters
2. Identify Key Players
3. Develop Work Plan

Phase II: Conduct Behavorial Interviews

1. Obtain Preliminary Information
2. Obtain Behavioral Information

Phase III: Construct Competency Model

1. Create Competency Dictionary
2. Create Competency Model

Phase IV: Assess Gaps

1. Identify Gaps
2. Analyze Results

Phase V: Implement Model

Following is an explanation of each phase and the corresponding steps within each.

Phase I: Develop a Project Plan

The purpose of this phase is to refine the scope and objectives for a project, create a project team, and establish a project management structure.

Establish Parameters

First it is essential to define how the competency model will be used. This can be done by conducting one-on-one interviews or a series of interviews with senior management. Following is a list of suggested questions that can be asked during these interview(s):

- What is the purpose of the competency study?
- How will the competency study meet the business needs of the organization?
- How many competency model(s) must be created: one job function (sales manager), a job family (sales associate, sales manager, sales executive), or multiple job families (production, systems, research and development)?
- Will the competency model(s) be used for other purposes, such as training, recruiting, performance management, or career planning?
- Are time and resources (such as personnel and budget) available?
- What additional resources will be required?
- What additional constraints are anticipated, such as deadlines or input from external customers?

Identify Key Players

It is also necessary to identify the people who will need to participate in a project. Depending on the scope, several players can be involved, including the following:

- Sponsor or decision maker,
- Steering committee,
- Project liaison,
- Human resource manager,
- Subject-matter experts,
- Internal or external customers,
- High performers,
- Target audience,
- Field personnel, and
- Training professionals.

Most small to medium-sized projects require a sponsor, a group of high performers, the target audience, a human resource manager, field personnel, and a training professional. Large-scale projects may also require the involvement of a steering committee and project liaison person to coordinate and administer a project. Subject-matter experts are needed when the job content for developing a competency model is highly technical and complex terms must be translated.

High performers are the star performers within an organization. High performers are the main source of information about the behaviors and actions that are necessary to do a job successfully. Following are a few guidelines for identifying high performers:

- People who consistently exceed expectations and achieve "very good" to "excellent ratings on company performance reviews,
- People who consistently meet or exceed business and unit objectives,
- People informally labeled "masters" or experts by their peers and managers—people who are sought for their knowledge of or expertise in a particular subject,
- People who like what they are doing, and
- People who are respected by others, which is particularly important in organizations in which close teamwork is necessary.

Usually, human resource personnel and managers can identify high performers within an organization.

Develop a Work Plan

After key players have been identified and their availability determined, the next step involves developing a work plan. Figure 4.1 shows a sample high-level work plan for two hundred people. To scope out tasks on a more detailed level, use Toolkit Form 4.1. (See the partially completed example in Figure 4.2.) After a project plan has been put into place, you can begin the data-collection process.

Phase II: Conduct Behavioral Interviews

The next step involves gathering data for building a competency model. Several methods, such as questionnaires or surveys, focus groups, and observations, can be used. By and large, one-on-one or group interviews have been shown to be the most effective method of obtaining behavioral data for competency-based assessments.

The main advantage of group interviews over individual interviews is that they are much faster. Important prerequisites for conducting interviews are good facilitation skills (if the group interview method is used) and the ability to develop and ask effective questions. This chapter focuses on how to use behavioral interviews as the primary data-collection method.

Behavioral interviewing is a technique that is adapted from Flanagan's Critical Incident Method (Flanagan, 1954). The basic purpose of behavioral interviews is to seek two types of information from high performers:

- Background and job-related information, and

- Information about what high performers do that makes them successful in their jobs.

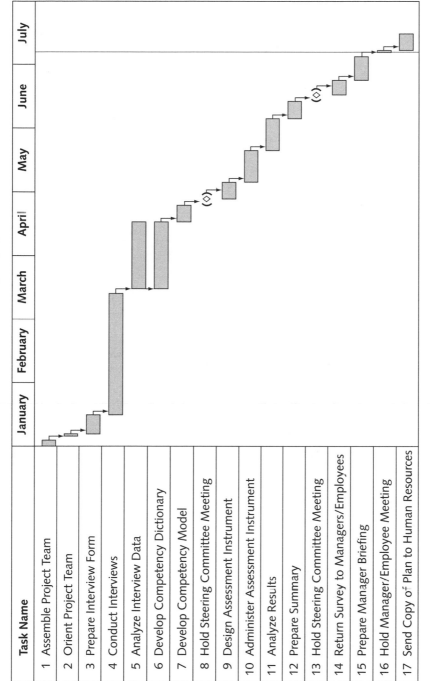

Schedule of Events - Overview (Sample)

Task Name	January	February	March	April	May	June	July
1 Assemble Project Team							
2 Orient Project Team							
3 Prepare Interview Form							
4 Conduct Interviews							
5 Analyze Interview Data							
6 Develop Competency Dictionary							
7 Develop Competency Model							
8 Hold Steering Committee Meeting							
9 Design Assessment Instrument							
10 Administer Assessment Instrument							
11 Analyze Results							
12 Prepare Summary							
13 Hold Steering Committee Meeting							
14 Return Survey to Managers/Employees							
15 Prepare Manager Briefing							
16 Hold Manager/Employee Meeting							
17 Send Copy of Plan to Human Resources							

FIGURE 4.1 *Competency Assessment Project Plan*

TOOLKIT FORM 4.1 *Competency Project Plan Worksheet*
Detailed Schedule of Events

Task	SC	HRM	SM 1	TP	PL	SM 2	C	Completion Date
8.0 Steering Committee Meeting								
8.1 Conduct meeting				4	4			4/30
8.2 Participate in meeting	4	4	4			4	4	4/30
8.3 Prepare meeting summary					8			5/1
Subtotal: (Hours)	4	4	4	4	12	4	4	

Project Members: (Enter names of project members here)

Key: SC = Steering Committee   HRM = Human Resource Manager   SM1 = Sales Manager 1
TP = Training Professional   PL = Project Liaison   SM2 = Sales Manager 2   C = Client

FIGURE 4.2 *Sample Toolkit Form 4.1: Competency Project Plan Worksheet*

The next two sections outline the steps for obtaining both these types of data.

Obtain Preliminary Information

In the beginning, it is essential to establish the right tone for an interview. A few techniques for doing this include building rapport, maintaining a neutral attitude, and so forth. Other guidelines for preparing and conducting interviews were explained in Chapter Two. Following is a sample script[1] that you can use to start developing your actual interview. Note that this script is appropriate for one-on-one interviews. However, it can also be modified and used for group interviews.

> Thank you for agreeing to participate in this study. As mentioned in the letter that you received last week, we are conducting a [name of job] competency study. The purpose of this study is to help [name of company] identify the competencies necessary for success in a [name of job] position.
>
> Over the years, you have become an expert at what it takes to be successful in this position, so [company name] would like to use your insights, as well as the insights of others like you, to create a best-practices model for [name of position].
>
> This model will be used in two ways. First, we will use the framework to improve the hiring and selection process for [name of position]. We will use the competency criteria identified from this study to select the right people for the job.
>
> Second, we will use the model to create a training program for [name of position]. We will also develop individualized programs to advance the skills of [name of position]. As you can see, this is a very important project, and management is committed to it.
>
> The format for collecting the information for this interview is fairly straightforward. I will ask you to think about several critical incidents that occurred during your work career in [name of field]. Then I will ask you to tell me two types of stories: those that describe major successes

---

[1] Adapted from *Competence at Work* by Lyle M. Spencer and Signe M. Spencer, © Copyright 1993 by John Wiley and Sons, Inc. Used by permission of John Wiley and Sons, Inc.

you experienced and those that resulted in not so successful outcomes. Before we discuss any of these incidents, I'd like to learn a little about you and your job.

After you have completed this preliminary introduction, you can give participants the opportunity to talk about themselves and their job responsibilities.

Obtain Behavioral Information

Following are sample questions for obtaining both job-related and behavioral information. For a sample interview worksheet see Toolkit Form 4.2 in the Toolkit section of the book.

1. What are the five main responsibilities of your job? *[Probe for quantifiable results such as, "Meet sales quota every quarter."]*

2. What skills and abilities do you need to accomplish each of these responsibilities? *[Probe for quantifiable behaviors and actions such as, "Make five new cold calls per month."]*

3. What other skills and abilities do you require to make you successful in your job? *[Probe for behaviors and actions such as, "Be courteous to customers."]*

4. Think about an incident you experienced that resulted in a successful outcome. What was the context? When did it happen? Who was involved? *[Probe for behaviors and actions such as, "Took the initiative, made quick decisions, listened carefully."]*

5. What did you feel or think? *[Probe for behaviors and actions such as, "I felt empowered."]*

6. What did you say? Why were these actions and words effective? *[Probe for behaviors and actions such as, "I took the initiative to authorize the shipment of several cartons of tape with an overdue shipment. This pleased the customer."]*

7. What were the results? What significance does this event have?

[Probe for behaviors and actions such as, "I learned that by acting quickly and decisively, I saved the company from losing a customer."]

During the next round of questions, ask interviewees to describe an event that resulted in *unsuccessful* outcomes. Most interviews take between two and two-and-a-half hours to complete. Learning to develop effective follow-up questions during an interview takes time and experience. There is no comprehensive list that is appropriate for all interviews. However, a few suggested phrases are given below that you can use as prompts:

- Describe for me. . . .
- Tell me about a time when. . . .
- Tell me about a situation that. . . .
- Can you be more specific about . . . ?
- Can you give me an example of . . . ?
- What specifically happened next?
- What was your response?
- What did you think when . . . happened?
- When you said . . ., what did you mean?
- I'd like to hear more about. . . .

Pitfalls To Avoid

The key to successful outcomes is also to avoid the following pitfalls:

- *Using the Wrong Questions.* For example, asking interviewees to justify, explain, or rationalize their behavior or asking leading questions;
- *Encouraging Guesses.* For example, asking interviewees to guess or anticipate their future actions or reactions or asking interviewees to guess or anticipate how others may act or react;

- *Using Ineffective Responses.* For example, encouraging responses through your body language, intonations, or comments, inaccurately paraphrasing an interviewee's comments, or interrupting the interviewee with questions; and

- *Making Assumptions.* For example, jumping to conclusions without knowing the facts or anticipating an interviewee's next steps.

Phase III: Construct Competency Model

After you have completed the interview process, start creating a preliminary draft of a competency model. This phase involves two steps: creating a *competency dictionary* and creating a *competency model.*

Create Competency Dictionary

First, identify similarities and patterns in data. Then group or chunk this information into themes or core clusters. For example, if the majority of responses indicate that articulation is an important interpersonal skill for sales associates, then "articulation" becomes a core cluster.

To create a dictionary, continue this chunking process until every core cluster has been defined. Review and edit definitions until you are satisfied with them. Finally, write an overall statement that describes each dimension, as shown in the sample of Toolkit Form 4.3 presented in Figure 4.3, which shows the dimension as "Interpersonal." Interpersonal is defined as, "Projects an attitude that is positive, perceptive, and sensitive to audience needs."

Create Competency Model

Figure 4.4: Sample Toolkit Form 4.4 shows a competency model for the job family "sales." The model is essentially a high-level depiction of the core elements contained in the dictionary: dimensions and core clusters. After the first draft of the competency model has been created, obtain approval from senior management and/or the human resource department. If necessary, make additional changes to the dictionary and the model based on their feedback. Then prepare a final copy.

TOOLKIT FORM 4.3 *Competency Dictionary—Sales*

---

1. *Leadership:* Uses the company vision to help others achieve personal and organizational goals.

Core Clusters	Definitions
Coaching	Assists others to advance their knowledge and skills by providing advice, encouragement, and feedback.
Influencing	Uses authority and personal charisma to gain support and commitment for goals.
Vision	Recognizes future opportunities for the organization and establishes long-term goals to maximize the potential.

2. *Interpersonal:* Projects an attitude that is positive, perceptive, and sensitive to audience needs.

Core Clusters	Definitions
Articulation	Expresses facts and emotions with clarity; generates an interest in the audience.
Listening	Uses active listening skills to understand the audience's point of view and to improve communication.
Self-Awareness	Is aware of how his/her personal actions and attitudes affect others; is perceptive and understands own strengths and weaknesses.

3. *Knowledge of the Industry:* Maintains an up-to-date understanding of the industry by reading industry journals, attending meetings and conventions, and networking.

Core Clusters	Definitions
Product and Service Knowledge	Understands the benefits, features, availability, and cost structure of the company's products or services.
Market Knowledge	Is familiar with the competition's products and services and how they compare to the company's products and services.

4. *Management:* Uses company resources and personnel to meet or exceed company goals.

Core Clusters	Definitions
Decision Making	Arrives at decisions by considering company goals, staff opinions, available resources, and potential consequences.

FIGURE 4.3 *Sample Toolkit Form 4.3: Competency Dictionary—Sales*

TOOLKIT FORM 4.3 *Competency Dictionary—Sales* (continued)

Core Clusters	Definitions
Budget Control	Manages expenses and controls cost within the company's expectations and projections.
Staffing	Anticipates staffing needs; selects, hires, develops, evaluates, promotes, and terminates staff according to company needs and individual performance.
Team Building	Encourages participation, creates common goals, facilitates interactions, recognizes individual contributions, monitors progress, and provides feedback.

5. *Sales Skills:* Meets or exceeds sales goals by anticipating and responding to clients' needs for services and products.

Core Clusters	Definitions
Prospecting	Recognizes potential clients and actively seeks new business opportunities.
Presentation	Establishes rapport easily; projects a positive, professional image; directs the conversation for results.
Persuasion	Effectively uses product knowledge, industry awards, client testimony, negotiation skills, and incentive programs to promote sales.
Customer Service	Seeks to improve customer satisfaction by anticipating and fulfilling the customers' needs and providing ongoing quality support and service.

6. *Personal Attributes:* Possesses values, attitudes, qualities, and behavior that are consistent with the industry and the organization's standards.

Core Clusters	Definitions
Initiative	Actively seeks and recognizes opportunities for improvement and growth; is creative and overcomes obstacles to reach goals and exceed expectations.
Integrity	Possesses principles and values and demonstrates behavior that is consistent with industry and company standards.
Flexibility	Adjusts positively to changes in the work environment and resources.

FIGURE 4.3 *Sample Toolkit Form 4.3: Competency Dictionary—Sales* (continued)

TOOLKIT FORM 4.4 *Competency Model—Sales*

Dimensions	Sales Associate	Sales Manager	Sales Executive
	Core clusters		
1. Leadership Uses the company vision to help others achieve personal and organizational goals.	Influencing	Coaching Influencing	Coaching Influencing Vision
2. Interpersonal Projects an attitude that is positive, perceptive, and sensitive to audience needs.	Articulation Listening Self-awareness	Articulation Listening Self-awareness	Articulation Listening Self-awareness
3. Knowledge of the Industry Maintains an up-to-date understanding of the industry by reading industry journals, attending meetings and conventions, and networking.	Product and service knowledge Market knowledge	Product and service knowledge Market knowledge	Product and service knowledge Market knowledge
4. Management Uses company resources and personnel to meet or exceed company goals.	Decision making	Decision making Budget control Staffing Team building	Decision making Budget control Staffing Team building
5. Sales Skills Meets or exceeds sales goals by anticipating and responding to clients' needs for services and products.	Prospecting Presentation Persuasion Customer service	Presentation Persuasion Customer service	Presentation Persuasion Customer service
6. Personal Attributes Possesses values, attitudes, qualities, and behavior that are consistent with the industry and the organization's standards.	Initiative Integrity Flexibility	Initiative Integrity Flexibility	Initiative Integrity Flexibility

FIGURE 4.4 *Sample Toolkit Form 4.4: Competency Model—Sales*

Phase IV: Assess Gaps

After a best-practices model has been built, you can measure gaps in proficiencies of others in the same job function(s). It is only after these gaps have been identified that appropriate interventions can be developed to close them. This phase consists of two steps: *identifying gaps* and *analyzing results.*

Identify Gaps

As explained in Chapter One, a gap is the difference between an actual situation and an ideal situation—the difference between what performance is and what performance should be. Surveys are an effective tool for gathering this type of data. The following example shows how a simple rating scale can be used to obtain information. Note that an actual survey would have the competencies identified from the analysis listed in the left-hand column.

SAMPLE SURVEY QUESTIONS

Instructions: Given the following rating scale, circle the number that corresponds most closely with the degree to which you agree or disagree with each statement.

1 = Strongly Disagree, 2 = Disagree, 3 = Neutral,
4 = Agree, 5 = Strongly Agree, N.A. = Not Applicable

Coaching: Assists others to advance
their knowledge and skills by
providing advice, encouragement,
and feedback.   1   2   3   4   5   N.A.

Influencing: Uses authority and
personal charisma to gain support
and commitment to goals.   1   2   3   4   5   N.A.

Analyze Results

After surveys have been distributed and returned, data can be analyzed by using any of the software packages that are available for this purpose or can be tabulated by hand.

Phase V: Implement Model

Competency models have many applications. They can be used to create individual employee learning development plans and also can be used to develop selection, hiring, and other performance management systems. This section will discuss one application: using individualized learning development plans after a competency model has been built.

After managers have received a copy of their employees' completed surveys, a brief meeting can be held with managers to explain how the learning development plans can be used. During this meeting, copies of the form can also be distributed (use Toolkit Form 4.5). A suggested agenda that managers can use to conduct an actual meeting with their employees is given below:

1. Review individual areas of strengths and identify opportunities for development.

2. Identify the support and resources necessary to facilitate performance.

3. Develop an action plan that best meets the needs of the learners.

4. Make a schedule for implementing learning development activities.

5. Discuss a follow-up plan.

After a model has been implemented, results can be monitored both at the organizational and individual level. At an individual level, managers can conduct quarterly or annual progress checks with their employees. At an organizational level, the impact of the assessment can be measured through client satisfaction surveys.

The preceding sections presented the methods and tools for doing a competency-based assessment. Now let us see how it was actually done at Midsize Community Savings Bank.

CASE STUDY AND TOOLS

The information for this case was contributed by Anne Marie Dyckman, Director of Human Resources at Midsize Community Savings Bank. This case shows the approach that was used to develop a competency model for branch managers. Although most events are real, a fictitious bank name has been used. The key tools shown here are the competency dictionary and the competency model. Highlights of the case are presented below.

———————

Midsize Community Savings Bank is a commercial bank with over $1B in assets. It is also a Federal Deposit Insurance Commission (FDIC) state-chartered bank. Historically a mortgage bank, the bank later changed to commercial lending activities. The bank has eighteen branch locations, each headed by a branch manager. Only sixteen branch managers participated in the competency study.

The Need

The president of the bank recognized that branch managers required a core set of competencies in order to be effective. It was also recognized that managers possessed these competencies, but to differing degrees. Further, the bank president wanted to establish a standardized method for selecting new candidates for the branch manager position.

A competency model would provide a tool for developing a model of best practices for branch managers. It would also help to create a training curriculum and aid senior management in making better choices when hiring new candidates.

The Approach

The project-planning and competency-modeling processes for Midsize Community Savings Bank were divided into four phases:

Phase I: Develop Competency-Model Strategy
Phase II: Gather Data
Phase III: Build Model
Phase IV: Applications

The steps undertaken in each phase are summarized below.

Phase I: Develop Competency-Model Strategy

1. The HR director met with the bank president and senior managers to determine the relationship of the project to business goals and strategies. It was decided that the HR director would work with management to determine business and measurement issues.

2. The HR director developed a project plan that included the size, scope, responsibilities, and time that would be needed to complete the project.

Phase II: Gather Data

1. The president of the bank and HR director identified the best possible sources of interview data. They also decided on the best candidates for the competency study.

2. The HR director interviewed selected individuals and obtained a detailed list of critical skills, abilities, and behaviors that made them successful branch managers. Candidates were asked to provide examples from their past that showed a specific time when a skill or behavior was used.

Phase III: Build Model

During this phase, the HR director completed the following steps:

1. Organized and ordered interview data by identifying similarities and patterns in behavioral data.

2. Prepared a draft of the completed template.

3. Edited content and grouped common themes.

4. Created competency definitions and developed a competency dictionary, as shown below.

5. Created the first draft of the competency model.

6. Presented the first draft of the dictionary and model to senior management.

7. Made the appropriate revisions.

8. Presented the final dictionary and model to senior management (see Figure 4.5 for the branch manager competency model.)

Dimension	Core Clusters			
1. Personal	Self-Confidence	Initiative	Achievement Orientation	
2. Thinking	Conceptual Thinking	Information Seeking	Creative Thinking	
3. Technical	Sound Business Understanding			
4. Relational	Customer-Service Orientation	Leadership	Interpersonal Understanding	Teamwork and Cooperation

FIGURE 4.5 *Competency Model: Branch Manager*

Phase IV: Applications

In the final phase, primary and secondary competencies for branch managers were identified. Primary competencies were those considered essential to success. These included self-confidence, initiative, achievement orientation, conceptual thinking, creative thinking, sound business understanding, customer-service orientation, and interpersonal understanding. Secondary competencies, such as information seeking, leadership, teamwork, and cooperation, were identified as competencies important to the job. See Figure 4.6 for more detail on the competencies measured.

The Results

A profile of a successful branch manager was developed, which then formed the basis for a new selection process. By using a five-item rating scale ranging from "very strong evidence skill is not present" to "very strong evidence skill is present," potential candidates were assessed on their ability to perform effectively in a branch manager position.

The competency model also served as the basis for a performance appraisal system. This was done using a seven-item Likert scale that ranged from 1 = Fails to 7 = Exceeds. In addition, a framework for training was also established.

CONCLUSION

Organizations must have effective ways to maximize human capital. Competency-based assessments offer one method for identifying and closing gaps in performance. Performance gaps can be measured more easily when an ideal model exists.

Competency modeling helps an organization define the knowledge, skills, abilities, and behaviors necessary for people to perform efficiently in their jobs. Many companies, such as General Electric, Digital Equipment Corporation, the Walt Disney Company, and Hallmark Cards,

Personal Cluster

A reflection of some aspect of an individual's maturity in relation to others and to work.

Self-Confidence	A person's belief in his or her own capability to accomplish a task; show independent judgment and act with self-assurance; carry out difficult assignments without supervision; and state own opinions clearly, even if supervisor disagrees.
Initiative	Take an independent action that involves doing more than is required or expected in the job; proactively prepare for competitive threats; act quickly and decisively in a crisis; and persist and refuse to give up when faced with obstacles or rejection.
Achievement	Set challenging goals, monitor progress orientation and make sure that results are achieved as planned; hold employees personally accountable for high standards of excellence in their work; and seek better, faster, more efficient ways of doing things.

Thinking Cluster

An understanding of and reflection on complex matters.

Conceptual Thinking	Identify the key aspects of complex situations and understand the big picture; see connections or patterns that are not obvious to others; understand how different problems, events, or concepts are related; and gain new insight from existing situations or old problems.
Information Seeking	An underlying curiosity or desire to know more about things, people, or issues; dig for exact information to resolve discrepancies by asking a series of questions; scan for potential opportunities that may be of future use; and personally go to see a loan applicant's business.
Creative Thinking	Develop imaginative solutions and new ways of thinking about solutions, problems, and opportunities; gain new insight by looking at situations from a different perspective; and create a climate for innovation and creativity by encouraging brainstorming in a safe and supportive environment.

FIGURE 4.6 *Competency Dictionary and Technical Cluster for Branch Manager*

Technical Cluster Function-specific knowledge and skills.	
Sound Business Understanding	Have an understanding of all business operations, including finance, marketing, product development, government regulations, business strategy, and seasonal trends; act as a business partner and/or advisor in business decisions. Provide insight to new-product development; act as a continuous source of information and insight into local competition; keep abreast of industry changes and developments, interpret business trends, and make sound decisions accordingly; and identify long-term business opportunities and encourage the bank to take advantage of them.
Relational Cluster Leadership, management, and interpersonal skills.	
Customer-Service Orientation	Possess a desire to help or serve both internal and external customers; encourage branch staff to treat other employees or departments as customers; seek information about the underlying needs of the customer beyond those expressed initially. Take personal responsibility for solving customer-service problems; act as a trusted advisor to customers; and work with a long-term perspective in addressing a customer's problems.
Leadership	Set a good example and inspire confidence, respect, and loyalty among staff; make oneself visible and accessible to staff and use informal contact to establish a climate of open communication; communicate confidence in one's own and others' abilities to meet goals and accomplish projects; motivate others to achieve by emphasizing their importance to the overall mission of the organization; and set branch goals or mission, even in the absence of clear direction from above.
Interpersonal Understanding	Able to understand the unspoken thoughts, feelings, and concerns of others; take time to listen to others' problems; accurately read the moods and feelings of others; and know what motivates specific individuals.
Teamwork and Cooperation	Possess a genuine intention to work cooperatively with others and to work together, as opposed to working separately or competitively; solicit ideas or opinions to help create buy-in; share all relevant and useful information; and credit others publicly for accomplishments.

FIGURE 4.6 *Competency Dictionary and Technical Cluster for . . .* (continued)

have used more comprehensive methods than those outlined in this chapter to develop models for improving managerial and organizational performance.

Competency modeling can be used in many ways. This chapter showed how individual learning development plans can be created after a model has been built. The case study described a bank's success in using the process to improve candidate selection, the performance appraisal system, and training for new and existing people in those positions.

This chapter described a process for identifying the competencies necessary for people to perform successfully in their jobs. The focus was on the individual. In the next chapter the focus will change to the job or task.

FIVE Job and Task Analysis

PURPOSE

This chapter will enable you to accomplish the following:

- Identify what a job and task analysis is;
- Recognize when to use one;
- Recognize benefits and drawbacks of the approach;
- Identify critical success factors for doing a job and task analysis;
- Identify key elements, including job responsibilities and job tasks;
- Examine three phases for conducting a job and task analysis;
- Identify shortcuts to the process; and
- Examine how a real-life job and task analysis was conducted at Boehringer Mannheim Corporation.

RELATED TOOLKIT JOB AIDS

The following job aids are available in the Toolkit section of this book:

- Job Analysis Questionnaire,
- Job Training Plan I (Professional/Supervisory/Management),

- Job Training Plan II (Administrative), and
- Job Task Analysis Checklist.

OVERVIEW

The prospect of undertaking a job and task analysis can seem formidable at first, but it is not as difficult as it appears. Usually, the analysis can be accomplished easily after you understand what it is and how it is done.

Job analysis is a process of gathering, organizing, evaluating, and reporting work-related information (Butruille, 1989). *Task analysis* is a method of determining the knowledge, skills, tools, conditions, and requirements needed to perform a job (Callahan, 1985).

The primary objective of a job and task analysis is to gather information about the scope, responsibilities, and tasks related to a particular job function or functions. This information is useful for an HRD practitioner because it helps in the preparation of job profiles or position descriptions. The position descriptions in turn serve as a platform for linking job requirements to current or future training needs.

Doing a job and task analysis not only helps people within an organization develop a clearer picture about what their jobs entail, but also helps them to understand what is expected of them. It also helps supervisors and managers establish criteria for job performance, which in a broader context lays the foundation for performance management and career planning systems.

The amount of time needed to complete a job and task analysis can vary from a few days to several months. How much time is taken depends on the number of job analyses and corresponding curriculum plans that must be developed.

WHEN TO USE

A job and task analysis is most effective under the following circumstances:

- When new or existing job descriptions or position profiles for managerial and nonmanagerial jobs must be developed as part of a performance management system,

- When jobs must be redesigned and tasks (knowledge, skills, and abilities) for each job identified, and

- When a consistent set of training requirements must be created, especially those involving highly technical or specialized job functions.

BENEFITS AND DRAWBACKS

Conducting a job and task analysis has several *benefits* for the organization:

- It stimulates buy-in and interest because people are directly involved in defining their jobs;

- It provides supervisors with a profile of skill sets that are necessary in order for people to perform competently in a given job function;

- It serves as a basis for distinguishing the skill requirements for various job classifications within a job category (such as entry-level versus senior positions);

- It serves as a benchmark for determining what additional knowledge, skills, or abilities must be acquired in order for people to move laterally across or upward within a job category; and

- It helps in the overall growth and professional development of people within an organization.

There are also some *drawbacks* to the approach:

- It does not take into account any external factors that may have an impact on job performance;

- It takes time and commitment; and

- It is costly.

CRITICAL SUCCESS FACTORS

A few factors are crucial to the successful completion of a job and task analysis project or initiative:

- Support from management,

- The availability of both human and monetary resources,

- A stable environment (it is difficult to question people about their jobs during downsizing, mergers, or takeovers), and

- Communication about what is being done and how it will impact people.

Both an organization and its people have much to gain from a job analysis, given the right tools and the right environment. First, we will begin by defining a few key terms. Next, some basic guidelines for writing effective job task statements will be presented because this is an important aspect of the process. Following this, the steps for doing a job and task analysis will be discussed.

Before we examine the steps for doing a job and task analysis, let us review a few terms that will be used in the chapter.

- *Job Responsibility.* Describes the scope of activities for a job function or job position, such as an operations manager, for example: Ensure that staff participate in the annual corporate professional education program; and

- *Job Task.* Describes what must be done in order to fulfill a responsibility. Usually there are four to six tasks for each responsibility, for example: Write an annual professional education program for each staff member.

WRITING JOB TASK STATEMENTS

Most people are familiar with the term "responsibilities." As a supervisor, one of your responsibilities may be to manage people. Another responsibility may be to conduct performance reviews. Each responsibility is comprised of several job tasks. A job task statement essentially describes the what, why, and how of a job, as shown in the example below.

What	Type a report
Why	To document the minutes of a meeting
How	By using a word-processing program

In general, it is useful to follow a few basic rules when writing job task statements:

- Avoid using negatives such as "will not participate in the fund-raising campaign";

- Avoid using jargon; and

- Restrict sentences to one idea.

In addition, job task statements should always begin with a specific verb. Following are a few suggested verb substitutes. For instance:

INSTEAD OF	CONSIDER USING
Communicate	Write, speak
Gauge	Evaluate, identify, measure, assess, determine
Strive	Accomplish, meet, conduct
Promote	Maintain

See the following statements and how they have been rewritten so that they begin with a specific action verb:

1. Work under direction of supervisor to develop an employee pension plan.

   Write an employee pension plan under direction of supervisor.

2. Interface monthly with business unit heads.

    Meet monthly with business unit heads.

3. Interact with treasury department to support implementation of new credit policy.

    Conduct weekly meetings with treasury department to support implementation of new credit policy.

4. Serve as lead for presentation of updated tariff policy plan.

    Lead the presentation on the updated tariff policy plan.

Standards

Occasionally, job task statements contain another component—a standard—at the end of the statement. A *standard* is a criterion that specifies how a task should be performed. For example:

- Correctly calculate the number of home closings per quarter;
- Monitor implementation of corrective action policy by reporting employee deviations to management; or
- Process new claims courteously in ten to fifteen minutes.

A more detailed example follows.

ASSEMBLY OF HELP DESK MANUALS

Task Statement	Assemble help desk manuals.
Standards	Make twenty copies of each 100-page binder using a copier, without assistance, within five business days. Insert five tab dividers in each binder in the proper order.

Usually, it is easier to specify standards for administrative and technical jobs because the degree of accuracy required for job performance is high, but because of the additional time required to obtain and prepare this data, the amount of time taken to complete a job and task analysis is longer. Now let us examine the phases and steps involved in a job and task analysis.

KEY PHASES

There are three stages in conducting a job and task analysis:

Phase I: Prepare
1. Identify High Performers
2. Prepare Job Analysis Questionnaire
3. Prepare Materials

Phase II: Conduct Job Task Analysis Work Session
1. Refine Job Responsibilities
2. Identify Job Tasks
3. Identify Training Requirements

Phase III: Implement Job Training Plan

Following is an explanation of each phase and the steps within each.

Phase I: Prepare

This phase consists of several tasks. First, assemble a project team. Depending on the scope of your project, a team can consist of yourself and a facilitator (to lead a job and task analysis work session, which is explained in more detail in Phase II), or it can include field personnel and subject-matter experts too. For high-profile projects, an advisory committee or expert panel may also be necessary.

Identify High Performers

Next, select four to six key people considered above-average to high performers in the job category being analyzed. The criteria for selecting high performers was explained in Chapter Four (see page 69). Occasionally, job function experts can also be used instead of high performers. Use job function experts when the job being analyzed is very technical or specialized.

During this preparatory stage, also inform participants that they have been selected to provide input for a job and task analysis session. Also inform participants' supervisors. For employees located in other branch offices or regions, make travel and other related arrangements. Also brief participants about the process if necessary.

Prepare Job Analysis Questionnaire

Figure 5.1, Sample Toolkit Form 5.1, shows a sample job analysis questionnaire that can be used to obtain job-related information prior to a focus group or work session. A week before the scheduled date of the session, distribute or mail these questionnaires to participants. This step not only helps participants begin thinking about the critical tasks involved in performing a job, but stimulates interest in the job and task analysis process as well.

Prepare Materials

After questionnaires have been returned, spend some time reviewing them. Later, transcribe key job responsibilities from questionnaires onto flip-chart paper. An example is shown on the following page.

Also prepare an agenda for the work session and make the appropriate number of copies (see Figure 5.2 for a sample agenda).

Before the session, gather appropriate materials, including the pre-prepared flip charts, questionnaires, copies of the agenda, blank flip charts, and markers. Also make arrangements for a meeting room. When setting up the room, post the pre-prepared flip chart in a prominent place.

EMPLOYEE	PRIMARY JOB RESPONSIBILITIES
Sue	**1.** Execute marketing and strategic initiatives for asset management group.
	2. Develop advertising, direct mail, customer communication, and public relations program for asset management group products.
John	**1.** Manage product development, competitive pricing analysis, and reporting for asset group products.
	2. Implement strategic and marketing programs worldwide for asset management group.

Phase II: Conduct Job Task Analysis Work Session

A job task analysis session requires good group facilitation techniques to elicit information from participants. The primary objective of a session is to identify the key responsibilities and job tasks needed for effective on-the-job performance. Once this information has been obtained, it can be used to further define the training requirements for a job.

Refine Job Responsibilities

The first task during a session is to obtain consensus from participants about the key responsibilities involved in performing their jobs. Refine the list of job responsibilities posted on the pre-prepared flip chart by combining similar statements. For example, Sue's first statement and John's second statement from the earlier example can be rewritten as follows:

> Execute marketing and strategic initiatives worldwide for asset management group.

Identify Job Tasks

Next ask participants to use the information from the questionnaires completed prior to the session to brainstorm a list of tasks for each job

TOOLKIT FORM 5.1 *Job Analysis Questionnaire*

Purpose: The purpose of this questionnaire is to gather information about your job.

Directions: Answer all the questions. Return the questionnaire to your supervisor

by _____ .

Sample Questions:

1. List all your major responsibilities. Then prioritize each item by assigning a number to it. For example, assign the number "1" to the responsibility you consider the most important.

   Develop data record layouts, input forms, record formats, testing schemes and test data. 1
   Write computer programs using logic flow charts, record layouts, and record
   formats.   2
   Ensure program accuracy by creating test programs, conducting spot checks, and
   reviewing output.   3

   Document programs, operations, and projects in accordance with company standards.   4

   Assist computer operations personnel with implementation of programs.   5

2. Why are these responsibilities important to your job?

   I need the specifications from the project lead to ensure that the logic programs and

   operating techniques I produce are efficient. I use the software programs and manu-

   facturer routines in areas of sort, utility, and bulk media conversion. I require a PC for

   documentation and program development and the disk storage device for creating

   permanent files.

3. What equipment and tools do you use in your job?

   PC computer, disk storage device, software programs, computer manufacturer routines,

   and job flow specifications from the project leader.

4. Describe some specific duties or tasks that you perform in your job. Next to each item, state how often you perform this duty or task.

   I review and evaluate job flow specifications to make sure that they are clear and that the

   project can be completed in the specified time. I do this about every three months. I write

FIGURE 5.1 *Sample Toolkit Form 5.1: Job Analysis Questionnaire*

or modify computer programs almost daily. I assist operations with the implementation of programs about once a week.

5. What knowledge do you require to perform your job successfully?

I need to know about accounting and manufacturing systems and data management techniques, and have some understanding of communication concepts.

6. What qualities are necessary to make you successful in your job?

I need to be able to work in a fast-paced environment and meet deadlines. I need to have good interpersonal skills to work with project leaders and operations personnel. I also need to be detail-oriented and care about quality control.

7. What prior knowledge, skills, or abilities did you bring to your position that helped to make you successful in your job?

To be successful in this job takes either a college degree or one or more years of programming experience. You need to be aware of the latest techniques in data processing, especially if it affects programming.

8. List any courses, workshops, or training programs you attended in the past that you feel have helped you succeed in your job.

I took a Myers-Briggs® course last year that helped me understand myself and others better. It made it easier for me to work with and understand the project leaders. I also completed a course in data management techniques, which was helpful because the field changes so frequently.

9. Describe any other contributing factors that you feel have made you successful in your job.

The systems project leader is very supportive. He helps me whenever I have a question or a problem with computer operations or data conversion personnel. He also lets me know where I stand and gives me feedback on my work.

FIGURE 5.1 *Sample Toolkit Form 5.1: Job Analysis Questionnaire* (continued)

Time	Activity
8:00 a.m. – 8:30 a.m.	Orientation • Introductions • Review purpose & significance of the session • Review agenda • Discuss "housekeeping" issues: breaks, lunch, phone, interruptions, protocol
8:30 a.m. – 10:00 a.m.	Refine list of responsibilities • Review prepared flip chart of responsibilities • Brainstorm additional responsibilities • Combine similar responsibilities
10:00 a.m. – 10:20 a.m.	Break
10:20 a.m. – 1:00 p.m.	Identify tasks for each job responsibility • Use data from questionnaires to brainstorm tasks • Review list and omit non-essential tasks
1:00 p.m. – 2:00 p.m.	Lunch Break
2:00 p.m. – 3:30 p.m.	Identify the knowledge, skills, and abilities and/or competencies required to perform each task.
3:30 p.m. – 4:15 p.m.	Identify training requirements necessary to acquire the knowledge, skills, and abilities and/or competencies for each task.
4:15 p.m. – 4:45 p.m.	Prioritize the training needs based on a consensus of the most critical tasks to job performance.
4:45 p.m. – 5:00 p.m.	Close • Review next steps in the process • Ask for subject-matter expert's availability for reviews • Thank participants

Note: The time required to complete the analysis may vary. An additional half day or day may be needed, depending on the complexity of the job responsibilities, the number of participants, and the facilitator's skills.

FIGURE 5.2 *Sample Agenda for Task Analysis Work Session*

responsibility. Post these on a flip chart. Ask the group to review the list of tasks. Have the group delete those tasks considered nonessential to the job. Ask participants to identify the knowledge, skills, and abilities required to perform each task by drawing on existing, prior, or on-the-job experience.

Identify Training Requirements

Also ask participants to identify the training necessary to acquire the knowledge, skills, and abilities for each task. A sample flip-chart page follows:

Position:	Project Leader
Job Responsibility 1	Manage multiple systems projects.
Job Tasks	Manage project schedules.
	Manage internal technical experts, project team, and vendors.
	Prepare interim and final reports.
Knowledge	Project management, software architecture
Skills and Abilities	Team leadership, resource management, oral and written communication skills.
Prerequisite Knowledge/Skills	UNIX, client-server systems, work flow/imaging implementation.
Training Required	Advanced project management, team management, writing business reports

Finally, ask participants to prioritize training needs based on tasks they consider most critical to job performance.

Phase III: Implement Job Training Plan

At this point, the data-collection process is complete. The next step is to review and organize the information obtained from the session. First prepare a preliminary draft; then present this draft to supervisors for review.

Ask supervisors to refine the list by adding or deleting tasks. After the draft has been approved, prepare a final copy of the job training plan. Figures 5.3 and 5.4 give sample job training plans for an administrative assistant and a marketing manager.

You may also need to obtain additional approval from the human resource department. After you have received approval from all the appropriate sources, present and distribute the final plan to senior management and the target audience. To facilitate this process, use the checklist provided in the Toolkit section, Form 5.4.

TIME-SAVING TIPS

A job and task analysis can be a time-consuming process. Following are a few ways to save some time during the process:

- Find existing copies of position descriptions from the human resource department if they are available. Use this information to draft your questionnaire. Asking more focused questions can reduce the amount of time spent in a work session.

- Ask job incumbents' supervisors to attend the latter portion of a work session. Ask them to review the preliminary draft of the job training plan developed by the group. Doing this not only eliminates one step in the process, but can reduce the amount of time spent in sending and waiting for a plan to be approved.

The previous sections presented the methodology and tools needed to perform a job and task analysis. Now, let us take a look at how the process was actually done at Boehringer Mannheim Corporation.

CASE STUDY AND TOOLS

The information for this case was contributed by Mary Keller, HR Consultant, Boehringer Mannheim Corporation. This case shows how a job and task analysis was used to develop a training plan for a Quality Control

TOOLKIT FORM 5.2 *Job Training Plan I*

Job Title: Marketing Manager
Department: Marketing
Location: New York

Job Responsibility 1: Develop Advertisements

1. Job Task: Define client needs

2. Job Task: Write ad copy

3. Job Task: Establish rapport with newspaper representatives

4. Job Task: Track ad response

5. Job Task: Manage advertising budget

Competencies: Grammar, understand the process of placing ads, math, organizational, ability to meet deadlines, interpersonal, word processing

Training Requirements: Features and process of writing advertisements, time management

Job Responsibility 2: Develop Direct Mail

1. Job Task: Write promotional materials, newsletters, pamphlets

2. Job Task: Identify potential audience

3. Job Task: Maintain database

4. Job Task: Evaluate vendor services and pricing structure

5. Job Task: Track response rate

Competencies: Grammar, math, market research, database management, analytical, computer

Training Requirements: Writing, database management, marketing, desktop publishing

Job Responsibility 3: Maintain and Develop Customer Communications

1. Job Task: Call customers once a quarter

2. Job Task: Respond to phone inquiries

3. Job Task: Mail appropriate materials to customers

4. Job Task: Request referrals

Competencies: Interpersonal skills, ability to handle multiple tasks, follow-through skills, product knowledge

Training Requirements: Time management, communication, product information, stress management

FIGURE 5.3 *Sample Toolkit Form 5.2: Job Training Plan I*

Job Responsibility 4: Develop Public Relations

1. Job Task: Attend Chamber of Commerce meetings

2. Job Task: Identify community charities

3. Job Task: Identify and participate in community activities

4. Job Task: Write articles for local newspapers

5. Job Task: Conduct presentations at schools, colleges, and professional meetings

Competencies: Grammar, community awareness, interpersonal, writing, assertiveness, presentation

Training Requirements: Assertiveness, writing, interpersonal skills, public speaking

---

Job Responsibility 5: Benchmark Company Performance

1. Job Task: Review competitors' materials

2. Job Task: Review industry literature

3. Job Task: Attend professional association meetings

Competencies: Knowledge of competition, awareness of industry publications, research techniques, analytical, interpersonal skills

Training Requirements: Communication, market research, interpersonal skills

FIGURE 5.3 *Sample Toolkit Form 5.2: Job Training Plan I* (continued)

TOOLKIT FORM 5.3 *Job Training Plan II*

Job Title: Administrative Assistant

Department: Accounting

Location: New York

Job Responsibility 1: Track Accounts Receivable

1. Job Task: Use spreadsheet to record accounts receivable

2. Job Task: Supply CFO with weekly summary report

3. Job Task: Contact delinquent accounts

4. Job Task: Reconcile ledger discrepancies

Knowledge: Accounting, math, knowledge of customer base

Skills/Abilities: Spreadsheet, word processing, interpersonal skills, organizational skills, attention to detail

Standards: Balanced accounts, timely and accurate reports, no accounts receivable balances over 45 days old

Training Requirements: Accounting, math, spreadsheets, word processing, time management

---

Job Responsibility 2: Pay Accounts Payable

1. Job Task: Review invoices for accuracy

2. Job Task: Rectify invoice discrepancies

3. Job Task: Balance payable accounts

4. Job Task: Prepare and mail payments

Knowledge: Accounting, math

Skills/Abilities: Attention to detail, spreadsheet, interpersonal skills, organizational skills

Standards: Accounts balanced, all discrepancies rectified, payments made within 45 days of the due date

Training Requirements: Accounting, math, spreadsheets, interpersonal skills, organizational skills

---

Job Responsibility 3: Prepare Financial Reports

1. Job Task: Review monthly records for accuracy

2. Job Task: Collect financial information for use in statistical analysis and business plans

3. Job Task: Prepare statistical summaries for management reports

4. Job Task: Duplicate and supply copies to senior management

FIGURE 5.4 *Sample Toolkit Form 5.3: Job Training Plan II*

Knowledge: Accounting

Skills/Abilities: Attention to detail, analytical skills, math, word processing, writing skills, time management, operation of the copy machine

Standards: Accurate, readable, and timely reports provided to all senior managers

Training Requirements: Accounting, company standards and practices, word processing, writing skills, time management, copy machine operations

Job Responsibility 4: Assist CFO with Communications

1. Job Task: Prepare memos

2. Job Task: Prepare meeting summaries

3. Job Task: Monitor e-mail, internal mail, and direct inquiries

4. Job Task: Handle phone calls

Knowledge: Phone and e-mail systems, names and positions of company personnel

Skills/Abilities: Writing skills, word processing, organizational skills, interpersonal skills

Standards: Memos and reports are concise, understandable, and timely. E-mail, internal mail, direct inquires, and phone calls are handled professionally.

Training Requirements: Writing skills, word processing, phone system, e-mail, internal mail systems, organizational skills, interpersonal skills

Job Responsibility 5: Track Sales Force Activity

1. Job Task: Review sales reports, compare actual sales with forecast sales

2. Job Task: Review sales expense and compare with budget

3. Job Task: Charge expenses to appropriate customer or product accounts

4. Job Task: Prepare monthly sales expense report

5. Job Task: Calculate sales bonus and commission compensation

Knowledge: Actual sales, forecast sales, budget allowances, knowledge of customer and product accounts, compensation rates

Skills/Abilities: Analytical skills, math, word processing

Standards: Monthly sales expenses are charged to appropriate accounts. Sales reports are accurate and prepared monthly. Bonuses and commissions are accurately calculated by last Friday of each month.

Training Requirements: Company financial reports, internal and external accounts, math, word processing

FIGURE 5.4 *Sample Toolkit Form 5.3: Job Training Plan II* (continued)

Inspector. The key tool shown here is the end product: a position training plan. Highlights of the case are presented below.

———————

Boehringer Mannheim Corporation (BMC) is a privately held worldwide health-care manufacturer. This biotechnology company has a diverse portfolio of "in vitro" diagnostic test systems, automated clinical chemistry systems, heterogeneous and homogenous testing, therapeutics, and biochemical products.

These products are used by physicians and life science research laboratories in many ways, including diabetes monitoring, patient sample analysis, and coagulation. BMC-West, located in Pleasanton, California, researches, develops, and manufactures medical diagnostic kits. This West Coast company employs about 270 employees.

The Need

As part of the requirements for obtaining ISO 9001 certification, the company had to meet the standard set by Element 4.19: Training. This element was one of twenty others in the 9001 standard. According to this specification, employees had to be qualified to perform their jobs. Documentation of their qualification was also needed.

At BMC, this requirement was satisfied by putting in place a training record system, position training plans, updated resumes, and company-wide training programs. These were strategically linked with the business culture of the company.

The Approach

Before examining the job and task analysis approach used by BMC to develop its position training plans, let us review a few terms that were specific to BMC's situation.

A *position training plan* (PTP) is a matrix that lists the knowledge, skills, and abilities needed for an individual to perform a job. It also contains the training and development activities that are necessary for minimal competencies.

A *learning channel* is a way of acquiring knowledge, skills, and abilities. These are broad categories meant to help employees and managers create ways to facilitate learning and development. These include:

OJT	On-the-job training
A	Assignment or project
M	Mentoring or coaching
W	Workshop, class, or seminar
C	Continuing education
S	Self-directed study

To meet the requirements of a position training plan, an employee must successfully complete the training and development activities, show evidence of previous comparable training, or demonstrate proficiency on the job. The PTPs are used as a guide by managers to identify the competencies an employee needs and the suggested learning channels for acquiring those competencies.

Following is a summary of the steps in the job and task analysis process used at BMC to develop its position training plans.

Phase I: Prepare

1. The Human Resource and Quality Assurance Departments identified the jobs for which PTPs needed to be written. Production jobs were given priority, as these jobs had a higher possibility of being audited.

2. Job descriptions for the targeted jobs were completed. The descriptions included the responsibilities, scope of decision making, and knowledge, skills, and abilities (KSAs) for each job function.

Phase II: Conduct Job Task Analysis Work Session

1. Human resource consultants met with managers and supervisors in small groups to explain the function of the PTPs and how they would be developed.

2. The following process was used to develop the PTPs:

Managers worked on the PTPs for the specific jobs reporting to them.

- Each KSA from the job description was listed on the PTP;
- Managers then added to and refined the KSAs;
- One or more learning channels were listed next to each KSA, which allowed managers and job incumbents flexibility in how they went about acquiring the new skill or knowledge and also acknowledged that formal workshops or classes were not always the best way to acquire a skill; and
- Comments (such as a deadline for meeting a certain training requirement) were added.

3. The Human Resource Department reviewed and finalized the PTP drafts.

Phase III: Implement Job Training Plan

1. Managers and the Human Resource Department signed the final PTPs.

2. PTPs were made available to all employees on paper and electronically.

A sample PTP for a Quality Control Inspector is shown in Figure 5.5.

The Results

PTPs were created for fifty-nine nonexempt jobs in the company. Further, the requirements for ISO 9001 were met. A linkage was also made between job descriptions, PTPs, managers' requirements for job performance, and the training needed to develop the requisite skills for a job.

DEPARTMENT: OPERATIONS, QA/QC

Knowledge

Training/Education	Learning Channel	Comments
High school or equivalent	C	
Basic understanding of GMPs and their application to the job	OJT, W, C, M	
Advanced working knowledge of critical and noncritical chemical inspections	OJT, A, M	Demonstrates independent judgment. Resolves problems and makes decisions and recommendations within the advanced scope of inspection.
Advanced working knowledge of packaging materials inspection	OJT, A, M	
Advanced working knowledge of packaging line, filling line, and labeling line clearance	OJT, A, M	

List what is required in each of these areas for minimal competence in performing the job:

Knowledge
- Business
- Areas of Expertise

Approved by: _____ Date: _____

HR Approval: _____ Date: _____

FIGURE 5.5 *Quality Control Inspector Position Training Plan*

CONCLUSION

Job and task analysis is a powerful tool that HRD practitioners can use in developing workforce potential. The information that is obtained from this process can serve as an important link in the evolution of many other related human development endeavors.

A job and task analysis is particularly useful in industries for which jobs are highly technical or specialized. Many state and federal agencies, such as the U.S. Defense Contract Agency and the Department of Labor, have used the method successfully to develop standardized training requirements for their employees.

This chapter described a skill-based approach to needs assessment. It established a context for the process by defining key terms and concepts. A synopsis of a biotechnology company's experience with the process and its outcomes was also presented. The next chapter presents a conventional approach to needs assessment: training needs assessment.

SIX Training Needs Assessment

PURPOSE

This chapter will enable you to accomplish the following:

- Determine what a training needs assessment is;

- Know when to use a training needs assessment;

- Recognize benefits and drawbacks of the approach;

- Identify critical success factors for doing a training needs assessment;

- Examine the steps for doing a training needs assessment; and

- Examine how a fictitious training needs assessment was conducted at Packaged Delivery, Inc.

RELATED TOOLKIT JOB AIDS

The following job aids are available in the Toolkit section of this book for use with the material in this chapter:

- Training Needs Assessment Interview Guide,

- Skills Assessment Survey,

- Customer-Service Training Needs Assessment Questionnaire,

- Management Training Needs Assessment Questionnaire, and

- Training Needs Assessment Checklist.

OVERVIEW

As a human resource generalist for a medium-sized manufacturing company, you may need to implement a company-wide orientation program. Or as the training manager of a large health-care facility, you may need to develop a series of management training programs for supervisory staff. Before you launch any training program, you must usually gather information about the developmental needs of your target group(s).

By using a systematic approach, you can ensure that gaps in performance are identified correctly. Usually, only those performance improvement opportunities that are caused by lack of knowledge or skills can be improved through training. Performance deficiencies that occur because of lack of motivation or environmental problems require non-training interventions, such as changes in performance appraisal or reward systems.

When designing training programs, the roles of HRD professionals vary, but some of the more common responsibilities that HRD professionals must undertake include the following:

- Developing a training agenda,

- Developing a specific training program (course/module), and

- Developing a training curriculum.

A needs assessment provides the information that is usually necessary for designing training programs. The basic purpose of a training needs assessment is twofold:

- To identify the knowledge and skills that people must possess in order to perform effectively on the job, and

- To prescribe appropriate interventions that can close these gaps.

The amount of time spent on conducting needs assessments varies. Although the majority are performed in less than a month, a few take up to a year to complete.

WHEN TO USE

A training needs assessment is most likely to be useful under the following circumstances:

- When new business opportunities arise,

- When a new system or technology must be implemented,

- When existing training programs must be revised or updated,

- When new job responsibilities must be assumed by people,

- When jobs must be upgraded,

- When organizations undergo downsizing, or

- When organizations experience rapid growth.

BENEFITS AND DRAWBACKS

There are two main reasons to conduct a training needs assessment:

- It ensures that training programs are developed based on identified needs; and

- It is relatively easy to implement.

The main drawback to the approach is that it lacks the rigor of a strategic needs assessment, competency assessment, or job and task analysis.

CRITICAL SUCCESS FACTORS

The following factors must be present for the successful completion of a training needs assessment:

- Support, both human and monetary, from senior management and line staff,

- Buy-in from special interest groups, especially if the assessment is perceived by some as a threat to their jobs, and

- Availability of personnel for data-gathering purposes.

KEY PHASES

A training needs assessment is made up of five phases:

Phase I: Gather Preliminary Data

Phase II: Plan

Phase III: Perform Training Requirements Analysis
1. Develop Tools

2. Conduct Analysis

Phase IV: Analyze Data

Phase V: Prepare Report

Following is an explanation of each phase and the steps within each.

Phase I: Gather Preliminary Data

As mentioned earlier, deficiencies in human performance and changes in the work environment often trigger the need for training. For instance, managers in Company A may be outstanding coaches, but lack technical skills. Technical staff in Company B may not have problems operating Machine X because they are familiar with the procedures, but have problems operating Machine Y because it has recently been installed.

In either case, the first step in conducting a training needs assessment is to gather some preliminary information about the training needs of the target groups. Some sources that can be tapped for conducting this preliminary analysis include:

- Clients (internal or external),
- Senior managers,
- Target audience,
- Functional heads or managers of the target audience,
- Subordinates,
- Internal or external customers,
- End users, and
- Others (such as peers or technical support staff).

When interviewing these sources, it is usually best to hold individual meetings with from three to five people. However, if a key person is unavailable, then the same information can be obtained through a phone interview. In the case of Company A, the primary group could consist of a manager, subordinate, and senior manager. For Company B, information could be obtained from a technical staff person and a supervisor. It is critical that the perspectives of one or two key decision makers (such as senior managers) also be obtained at this stage. The objectives of this phase are listed below:

1. *Establish the goals of the assessment.* As the following example illustrates, the goals can differ in purpose and scope. It is therefore critical to clarify the purpose of an assessment up front, so that appropriate data can be collected.

- *Goal 1.* Determine the worldwide training needs of all Company Y technicians.
- *Goal 2.* Determine the training needs of all Company Y Level 1 and Level 2 technicians in the United States and Canada.

2. *Obtain a more holistic perspective about the training needs.* Use the questions from Toolkit Form 6.1. Answers to these questions can help to elicit a broad understanding about how lack of training is affecting workplace productivity. The second set of questions on the form can be used to develop a better understanding about what the assessment should accomplish.

In addition, use the checklist from Toolkit Form 6.7 to gather all the appropriate background information before starting an assessment. Potential obstacles that can arise when implementing an assessment and tips for overcoming them are presented in Figure 6.1. After all the necessary data has been obtained, summarize your findings in a brief report that contains the following:

- Statement of the problem,
- Situation analysis,
- Goals,
- Preliminary findings, and
- Next steps.

Phase II: Plan

The next step involves developing a work plan to ensure that you stay on target with your assessment. When preparing a work plan, seek the input of your client contact at the beginning, as this person usually has the best knowledge about the operations of his or her unit or group, peak business periods to avoid, and so forth. Following are some steps to take when planning an assessment:

Some of the most common obstacles that arise when conducting a needs assessment are listed below. An "O" denotes a potential obstacle. An "S" indicates a suggested solution.

O   Lack of consensus about goals.
S   Gain consensus by obtaining the input of a senior executive.
S   Revisit the business goals of the organization and ensure that the assessment ties in with them.

O   Support from senior management, but lack of support from line managers or supervisors.
S   Obtain buy-in from a line manager or supervisor who can influence other managers.
S   Seek the intervention of senior management and make the assessment a priority for middle managers.

O   Lack of a sponsor with authority.
S   Seek the support of someone else in a higher position.

O   Too much background information to review.
S   Revisit the goals of the assessment; establish priorities; and discard information that is not relevant to the assessment.

O   Conflict about types of data that must be collected.
S   Revisit the goals of the assessment.

O   Bias in favor of a particular instrument(s).
S   Show the benefits of other instruments.

O   Resistance to questioning from middle management or special interest groups (such as union members or line staff).
S   Promote awareness about the benefits of the assessment through informational meetings.

O   Lack of access to those working night shifts or people assigned to restricted work areas.
S   Find alternative personnel.
S   Obtain special permission to gather data.

FIGURE 6.1 *Barriers to Success and How To Overcome Them*

O   Disagreement among team members about the method to use to implement the assessment.
S   Seek the opinion of a third party such as a senior manager.

O   Lack of willingness on the part of people to change when implementing a new system or technology.
S   Create a change readiness program.

O   Attitude of "Who has the time to complete another survey?"
S   Obtain buy-in by having the president of the company or a senior manager endorse the process.
S   Explain benefits to users.
S   Offer incentives for completing the instrument.

O   Lack of buy-in to needs assessment results (especially negative or controversial findings).
S   Present alternatives to overcome negative or controversial findings.

FIGURE 6.1 *Barriers to Success and How To Overcome Them* (continued)

1. *Determine what types of data must be collected.* Usually, the goals that were established in the first phase set the stage for data-collection efforts in this phase.

2. *Determine sources of data.* For group sizes under thirty-two, include every person in your study. If your target audience includes groups and subgroups from different hierarchical or educational levels, then select a representative sample from each group. For more information on sample sizes, consult the book *Performance Consulting* by Robinson and Robinson (1995). In addition, use the following guidelines when making decisions about who to include in an assessment:

    • *When implementing a new system or technology,* involve technical or subject-matter experts, the target audience, supervisors, end users, and other related internal or external customers;

- *When doing a job skills assessment,* involve subject-matter experts, job incumbents, supervisors, and other related internal or external customers;

- *When revising or updating an existing program,* include the target audience, subject-matter experts (if required), supervisors, and other related internal or external customers; and

- *When developing a new program,* include the target audience, subject-matter experts (if required), supervisors, and other related internal or external customers.

3. *Determine the types of analyses that must be performed.* Figure 6.2 shows some of the common purposes of a training needs assessment. Usually, the specific business needs of an organization will determine whether any statistical analyses, such as averages or correlations, must be computed. As mentioned in Chapter Two, seek the expertise of someone with experience in statistics when preparing data-collection instruments.

---

1. Learner analysis
2. Subject-matter analysis
3. Comparison of knowledge levels: current versus desired
4. Comparison of skill levels: current versus desired
5. Attitude toward learning
6. Attitude toward change
7. Attitude toward existing training programs
8. Attitude toward a new system or technology
9. Quality of existing training programs
10. Problem solving

FIGURE 6.2 *Common Types of Analyses Performed in a Training Needs Assessment*

4. *Identify the types of tools that will be used to collect data.* Typically, using two or three different data-gathering methods increases the validity and reliability of data. For instance, you could supplement surveys with follow-up interviews or observations or use focus groups as your primary data-gathering tool and collect additional information through observation.

An overview, including the benefits and drawbacks of four primary data-gathering methods, was given in Chapter Two.

After you have completed the above steps, notify people involved about the plan through letters, the telephone, or e-mail and obtain approval to proceed with the assessment.

Phase III: Perform Training Requirements Analysis

A gap is the difference between what is and what should be. A training needs assessment helps to narrow this gap by identifying where performance deficiencies exist. The first two phases helped to lay the groundwork for an assessment. This third phase consists of two steps: developing tools and conducting the analysis.

Develop Tools

Because each organization's assessment requirements are unique, the best strategy is to follow the basic guidelines for preparing interview forms, questionnaires and surveys, and focus group questions discussed in Chapter Two. As a rule of thumb, allow about two days to prepare each instrument, but factor in additional time if special features must be built in.

Figures 6.3 and 6.4 are real-life examples of instruments that were used to measure gaps in skill proficiencies. Figure 6.3 is a simple self-assessment instrument that was used to monitor job activity levels at a major hospital. Figure 6.4 shows a portion of a performance skills profile that was used to assess the training needs of employees at an insurance company.

A blank form that can be customized is provided in the Toolkit section at the back of the book (see Toolkit Form 6.2). In addition, Toolkit

	Importance	Amount of Time Spent	Performance
	1 - Unimportant 2 - Minor 3 - Important 4 - Very Important 5 - Critical	0 - Never do this task 1 - Very little compared to other tasks 2 - Somewhat less compared to other tasks 3 - Same amount as other tasks 4 - More compared to other tasks 5 - A great deal more compared to other tasks	1 - Have low or no skill 2 - Perform well enough to get by 3 - Perform in this area without any problem 4 - Have a definite strength or high skill 5 - Have maximum skill

Instructions: For each task activity, circle the number corresponding to its importance for your job, the amount of time you spend on it, and how well you feel you perform it.

	Importance	Amount of Time Spent	Performance
Medicare Tape Run Edit Lists	1 2 3 4 5	0 1 2 3 4 5	1 2 3 4 5
Tape List Claims	1 2 3 4 5	0 1 2 3 4 5	1 2 3 4 5
Paper Claims	1 2 3 4 5	0 1 2 3 4 5	1 2 3 4 5
Sort Error Claims for Reviewers	1 2 3 4 5	0 1 2 3 4 5	1 2 3 4 5
Call on Medicare Tape Runs	1 2 3 4 5	0 1 2 3 4 5	1 2 3 4 5
Work All Railroad EOB's	1 2 3 4 5	0 1 2 3 4 5	1 2 3 4 5
Check All Payments	1 2 3 4 5	0 1 2 3 4 5	1 2 3 4 5
Review All Rejects	1 2 3 4 5	0 1 2 3 4 5	1 2 3 4 5
Resubmit With Correct Info.	1 2 3 4 5	0 1 2 3 4 5	1 2 3 4 5
Meet With Supervisor for Major Problems	1 2 3 4 5	0 1 2 3 4 5	1 2 3 4 5
Work on Groups	1 2 3 4 5	0 1 2 3 4 5	1 2 3 4 5
Call Patients to Correct Primary Insurance	1 2 3 4 5	0 1 2 3 4 5	1 2 3 4 5
Call Medicare to Update Insurance	1 2 3 4 5	0 1 2 3 4 5	1 2 3 4 5

FIGURE 6.3 *Job Activity Self-Assessment*

1. About You

Name: _____ Date: _____

a. Department: _____ Date of Employment: _____

Title of Current Job: _____

Objective of Current Job *(describe in 10 words or under)*: _____

_____

_____

b. What equipment do you routinely use in your current work? *(check all that apply)*

_____ telephone _____ computer (terminal) _____ PC

_____ typewriter _____ calculator _____ fax _____ copier

_____ microphone _____ other

c. List other equipment here:

_____

_____

_____

2. About Your Formal Education *(optional)*

Circle the highest scholastic level achieved: 11 or below, 12, 13,
14, 15, 16, 17, 18

3. About Your Work Experience

a. What *other* positions have you held *(list most current first)*

Title   Brief Description of Job Objective

_____

_____

_____

_____

_____

b. Equipment used in these jobs *(other than those listed above)*

_____

_____

FIGURE 6.4 *Performance Skills Profile*

4. About Your Computer Experience

Listed below are some of the most common computer applications used at our company.

In column A, rate your skill level in the application used in your current job.

In column B, rate your skill level in the application not used in your current job, but in which you possess prior experience.

If an item is not applicable, place a check mark in the NA column.

Use the following scale:

Not Confident	Somewhat Confident		Confident	Very Confident
1	2	3	4	5

A	B	NA		
_____	_____	_____	Keymaster BML	Keypunch
_____	_____	_____	Keymaster NY	New York Keypunch
_____	_____	_____	KDM1	Card Update Menu
_____	_____	_____	LBUP	List Bill Name and Address
_____	_____	_____	LCOO	Life Claim Payment
_____	_____	_____	LOTUS 123 (v.2.3)	Spread Sheet (old version)
_____	_____	_____	MDOC	MDO Coupon Update
_____	_____	_____	MIB	Medical Information Bureau
_____	_____	_____	MMOO	Mass Marketing
_____	_____	_____	NADU	MDO Name and Address Update
_____	_____	_____	NARE	Ordinary Life Underwriting
_____	_____	_____	NBOO	Ordinary Policy Issue Data
_____	_____	_____	Netware Utilities	Novell Application
_____	_____	_____	New Business	ESO Application
_____	_____	_____	NMCH	New York Complex Change
_____	_____	_____	NPAY	New York Payment Menu
_____	_____	_____	ORG PLUS	Organization Charts
_____	_____	_____	OSD1	BML Check Disbursement
_____	_____	_____	PACU	Pre-Authorized Checking Update
_____	_____	_____	Q&A	Data Base, Word Processor
_____	_____	_____	Schedule D	Securities, Financial
_____	_____	_____	SmartSuite	Five LOTUS Applications, as follows:
_____	_____	_____	123 (v.5)	Spread Sheet
_____	_____	_____	Approach (v.3.0)	Data Base
_____	_____	_____	Ami-Pro (v.3.1)	Word Processor
_____	_____	_____	Organizer (v2.1)	Personal Schedules
_____	_____	_____	Freelance (v.2)	Presentation Graphics
_____	_____	_____	Solomon	Accounts Payable
_____	_____	_____	UFND	Unclaimed Funds
_____	_____	_____	UPDT	Conservation/Coupon Entry
_____	_____	_____	VISIO	Flow Charts, Process, etc.
_____	_____	_____	Windows (v3.1)	User Interface
_____	_____	_____	WordPerfect	Word Processor
_____	_____	_____	ZEKE	Work Center Control

Please add below and rate those applications not listed above.

_____ _____ _____

_____ _____ _____

FIGURE 6.4 *Performance Skills Profile* (continued)

5. About Training Related to Your Occupation

List below *any* formal training you received *during the last five years* relating to any job you held *at any company*. List in sequence from most current.
Example: 9/95, Windows 3.1; 3/95, Basic keyboard skills; 10/94, Time management; etc.

Date	Name of Training Course		Date	Name of Training Course
1. _____			**5.** _____	
2. _____			**6.** _____	
3. _____			**7.** _____	
4. _____			**8.** _____	

(If you need more space, use a separate sheet and print your name.)

6. About Assessing Your Training Needs

a. Given your current duties, accountabilities, and position objectives, *assign two ratings to each of the items listed below.*

In column A, rate *your need* for training.

In column B, rate *its importance* to your job.

Provide a rating, as above, for any entry you make on the "Other" line.

If an item is *not applicable*, place a check mark in the NA column.

Use the following scale:

Very Low	Low	Average	High	Very High
1	2	3	4	5

A	B	NA	
			Communication Skills
___	___	___	**a.** Oral communication skills
___	___	___	**b.** Written communication (letters/memo/reports)
___	___	___	**c.** Formal presentation skills
___	___	___	**d.** Leading effective meetings
___	___	___	**e.** Other
			Customer-Service Skills
___	___	___	**a.** Telephone skills
___	___	___	**b.** Listening/questioning skills
___	___	___	**c.** Handling difficult customers and complaints
___	___	___	**d.** Other
			Performance Management Skills
___	___	___	**a.** Monitoring performance/correcting problems
___	___	___	**b.** Providing feedback/motivation
___	___	___	**c.** Coaching, counseling
___	___	___	**d.** Conflict resolution

FIGURE 6.4 *Performance Skills Profile* (continued)

Form 6.3, a customer-service training survey, and Toolkit Form 6.4, a management development questionnaire, are included to help you start to develop these types of assessments. Toolkit Form 6.4 also contains a management development survey that can be administered to managers' managers and/or subordinates to obtain their perspectives about managerial effectiveness. Following are some additional tips to consider when developing tools:

- Refer to the goals and objectives of your assessment;

- Include an *opening* (purpose and instructions for surveys and questionnaires and an overview or introduction for interviews and focus groups), *body* (questions), and a *closing* (demographic data, in the case of surveys and questionnaires, or appropriate closing remarks when conducting interviews or focus groups);

- Demarcate and label sections clearly;

- Include a key if a rating scale will be used (the most effective scales are five-point scales);

- When using two sets of rating scales per question, as shown below, seek the expertise of someone who can interpret the results accurately;

	PROFICIENCY					**IMPORTANCE TO JOB**				
	Very Low			Very High		Very Low			Very High	
Lotus 123	1	2	3	4	5	1	2	3	4	5

- Limit the number of questions so that interviews and focus groups can be conducted in about two-and-a-half hours and surveys and questionnaires can be completed in twenty-five or thirty minutes;

- Limit the number of items to be assessed in surveys and questionnaires. For instance, if you listed over fifty items and the majority received a rating of "3" or below (with the implication that training was needed), you would need to develop a training plan that could accommodate all these programs. Because most people attend an average of seven training programs per year, it could take several years to train everyone. A more effective strategy is to prioritize the items to be included in a survey or questionnaire, based on the most critical requirements for the job.

Conduct Analysis

After you have prepared your instruments, you are ready to begin the data-collection process. Toolkit Form 6.7 lists several factors to take into account when performing this step. Note that the checklist is designed as a guide. To optimize its use, complete only those items that are applicable to your particular situation. Following are a few additional tips to remember when conducting an analysis:

- When working in teams, ensure that everyone follows the same procedure;

- Limit the amount of time for returning surveys or questionnaires to ten days; and

- Have supervisors or managers follow up if instruments have not been received after ten days.

Phase IV: Analyze Data

After completing Phase III, you will have collected data from surveys or questionnaires, interviews, or focus groups. To analyze the data, use the process for compiling results that you selected in Phase II. The following are a few strategies for ensuring success in this phase:

- Limit responsibility for this task: Assume it yourself or delegate it to one or two individuals;

- Review data for discrepancies or deviations and present irregularities in data in a separate section;

- Always keep your client contact apprised of discrepancies in data;

- Omit extraneous or irrelevant data, for example, eliminate any information that does not pertain specifically to the assessment that you may have gathered while interviewing or while tape recording responses;

- List responses that do not fall into any category in a separate section titled "other";

- Establish codes for answers to qualitative data so that you can group responses into categories (for example, if the majority of responses to a question fall into three main categories, then assign a code such as A, B, or C to each category);

- Next to each category, list the frequency of responses (an example is shown below);

Q. Why do you think team training is needed?

Type of Response	Number of Responses
A. People don't know how to work in teams.	15
B. There is lack of cooperation among units.	10
C. There is lack of clarity about team roles.	11

- When faced with conflicting data, seek the opinion of an expert or individual(s) who are qualified to make a judgment.

Phase V: Prepare Report

The final step in a training needs assessment consists of preparing a formal report. The contents of these reports vary. But reports generally contain the following:

- Executive summary,

- Goals or objectives,

- Overview of data-collection methods,

- Findings or conclusions,

- Recommendations, and
- Appendix.

Given below are some guidelines for presenting conclusions and recommendations:

- Tailor the presentation style to the culture of your organization;
- Verify budgetary constraints so that recommendations are on target;
- Present recommendations in a matrix based on the following criteria: cost, urgency, availability of resources (monetary and nonmonetary), and feasibility;
- Research the feasibility of each recommendation thoroughly and offer alternatives;
- Use benchmarking data when available;
- Use a cost/benefit approach for the analysis (for an overview of how to do a cost/benefit analysis, see Darrough & Sharpe, 1997); and
- Support recommendations with citations from authorities in the field or industry "best practices."

If you are preparing a curriculum plan, the following is a suggested list of content areas to include:

- Overview,
- Statement of problem,
- Learner analysis,
- Detailed course objectives,
- Course outlines,
- Training schedule (quarterly, bi-annual, or annual),

- Training delivery strategy, and

- Evaluation strategy.

Toolkit Forms 6.5 and 6.6 can be used to develop high-level and detailed curriculum plans. Each type of plan can also include a core and/or advanced curriculum. Usually, core curriculums are more appropriate for beginning or intermediate learners. In addition, the checklist in Toolkit Form 6.7 can be used to ensure that all the key tasks for conducting a training needs assessment have been completed.

The previous sections presented the methodology and tools for performing a training needs assessment. Now, let us take a look at how it was done at a fictitious company, Packaged Delivery, Inc.

CASE STUDY AND TOOLS

The information for this case was contributed by Jeanne Strayer, a training and performance improvement consultant based in Oceanside, California. Although all events are real, a fictitious name has been used for the company at the request of the contributor. The case shows the approach used to conduct a needs assessment in preparation for a new company-wide training program. The key tool shown here is a set of interview questions used for lead drivers, first-line supervisors, and senior managers. Highlights of the case are presented below.

———————————

Packaged Delivery, Inc., is one of the largest packaged product delivery companies in the United States. It manufactures and distributes product through home and commercial delivery, as well as through retail outlets such as supermarkets. The company has six regions in ten states. Each region has between four and six branches. Each branch is responsible for delivering its product to customers on designated routes. Depending on the size of the branch, lead drivers may report to two or more sales supervisors.

The Need

Packaged Delivery, Inc., recognized that lead drivers were being asked to expand their job duties. Because of their seniority, leads were expected to coach and train their peers—those responsible for driving routes and delivering products. The leads benefitted because coaching offered a balance to driving, delivery, and bookkeeping duties. The company benefitted because leads often spotted and corrected performance problems with new trainees. Yet, leads did not necessarily have the skills to be effective trainers or coaches. Although they had sound technical skills, developing people was a different type of skill. The company saw the need for a program to help drivers learn to train and coach others.

The Approach

A five-phase approach was used to conduct the needs assessment. The following is a summary of the major steps and findings in each phase.

Phase I: Gather Preliminary Data

Preliminary data was gathered when the designated course developer met with the HR director and two regional vice presidents. The group confirmed the situation, but also pointed out some unique characteristics of the leads' situation that had to be addressed:

- Leads were placed in a position of responsibility, but had little or no authority;

- It was difficult for leads to find time to coach and train because their regular duties consumed so much time;

- Leads needed to strike the right balance between resolving problems behind the scenes and going to the supervisor if management intervention was needed, which was especially true with respect to union regulations; and

- Leads were often promoted within the same group with whom they were formerly peers, a situation that sometimes lead to new dynamics and tension.

Phase II: Develop a Plan

1. The group agreed on the scope of the training and the plan for the needs assessment. All operational leads in the company (approximately 110 people) would be trained. The needs assessment would involve interviews with members of the target audience, their supervisors, and selected HR personnel deemed experts in coaching skills and union practices.

2. The following goals were identified for the interviews:

- Determine the gap between the desired level of coaching skills and current level of skills;

- Assess leads' attitudes toward training; and

- Obtain real-life situations that could serve as examples, case studies, or role plays during classroom training sessions.

Phase III: Conduct Needs Analysis

1. Interview instruments were created for leads and their supervisors (see Figure 6.5).

2. Instruments were reviewed and approved by the HR director.

3. Interviews were conducted with fourteen leads, six supervisors, and two regional vice presidents. Interviews with supervisors and vice presidents confirmed the data collected from leads.

4. Interviews with HR personnel were helpful in determining the types of coaching and training skills needed for nonsupervisory positions. The interviews also provided valuable insight into the constraints faced by leads when working as union members.

Phase IV: Analyze Data

1. Recurring themes from qualitative data were noted and organized into categories. For example, responses to a question on obstacles to coaching on the job were grouped into three categories:

- Lack of time to coach,

Questions for Lead Drivers

1. According to the job description, a lead driver spends time training new hires and coaching experienced drivers as well as covering open routes. What percentage of your time do you estimate is spent on training and coaching?

2. What common performance problems do new hires have? Experienced drivers?

3. What sorts of situations call for coaching on your part?

4. What are the biggest challenges of a lead driver's job?

5. What were the biggest pitfalls you encountered as a new coach and trainer? What mistakes did you make at first? What lessons have you learned over time?

6. What do you do when someone is having trouble or not meeting standards? Do you have a standard procedure?

7. Can you tell me about a successful experience you have had in coaching someone?

8. Tell me about a not-so-successful experience you have had coaching someone? Why was it not successful?

9. How do you encourage and motivate other lead drivers? Do you use incentives or rewards? Do you try other things? (For example, pay compliments, recognize people, give personal attention.)

10. What keeps you from being a good coach on the job?

11. Have you received training in coaching or developing people?

12. Please rate yourself on the following skills on a scale of 1 (low) to 5 (high). These ratings are confidential and will not be attributed to any one person.
    a. Listening empathetically _____
    b. Giving directions clearly _____
    c. Giving feedback constructively _____
    d. Involving people, rather than telling them what to do _____
    e. Demonstrating a new skill in such a way that another person understands the critical aspects, e.g., does it correctly _____
    f. Guiding a team member to a solution for a problem _____
    g. Knowing how to recognize someone for a job well done _____
    h. Pointing out how someone's behavior is negatively affecting indicators and key measures _____

13. What topics would you like to see covered in training?

FIGURE 6.5 *Interview Questions*

Questions for Supervisors

1. According to the job description, a lead driver spends time training new hires and coaching experienced drivers, as well as covering open routes. What percentage of a driver's time do you estimate is spent doing training and coaching?

2. What are some of the skills you expect a lead driver to demonstrate as a coach or trainer? Do the lead drivers currently perform these skills? Why or why not?

3. What would the impact be on your branch if lead drivers were used effectively as coaches and trainers?

4. What kinds of situations call for coaching by drivers? What measures should be taken?

5. What is a common performance problem for a new hire? For an experienced driver?

6. What are the biggest challenges lead drivers face as coaches or trainers?

7. What are the biggest pitfalls you have seen new coaches fall into? What mistakes do they commonly make?

8. Do lead drivers have the skills to help *solve* a problem rather than just bring it to the person's attention? For example, can a lead driver come up with strategies to help someone increase sales, improve customer satisfaction ratings, etc.?

9. Think about the lead drivers who report to you now. How would you rate them on a scale of 1 (low) to 5 (high). These ratings are confidential and will not be attributed to any one person.
   a. Listening empathetically   _____
   b. Giving directions clearly   _____
   c. Giving feedback constructively   _____
   d. Involving people, rather than telling them what to do   _____
   e. Demonstrating a new skill in such a way that another person
      understands the critical aspects, e.g., does it correctly   _____
   f. Guiding a team member to a solution for a problem   _____
   g. Knowing how to recognize someone for a job well done   _____
   h. Pointing out how someone's behavior is negatively affecting
      indicators and key measures   _____
   i. Encouraging and motivating others   _____

FIGURE 6.5 *Interview Questions* (continued)

---

10. Does anything keep lead drivers from being good coaches on the job? Are there physical constraints, time constraints, or other factors?

11. Have lead drivers received any training in coaching or developing people?

12. What topics would you like to see covered in training?

Questions for Vice Presidents

1. How would you like to see lead drivers used as coaches and trainers for new hires?

2. What impact would the lead drivers make if used effectively as coaches or trainers? What key measures or indicators would be affected?

3. What are the biggest challenges lead drivers face on the job as coaches or trainers?

4. What would you like to see emphasized in a coaching skills program for lead drivers?

FIGURE 6.5 *Interview Questions* (continued)

- Physical environment (open cubicles, no privacy), and

- Personal reluctance to coach former peers.

2. The interviews also yielded quantitative data that helped determine deficiencies in participants' skills. Some of the items and their ratings included:

- Listening empathetically   3.2

- Giving directions clearly   3.2

- Giving feedback constructively   3.0

- Involving people rather than telling them what to do   2.5

All items that received a rating of 3.5 or under were earmarked for training.

Phase V: Write Report

1. A report was prepared for the HR director that summarized the results of the needs assessment and gave recommendations for the content, skills, examples, and issues to be covered during training. The report included a proposed outline of the training program, which not only incorporated all the recommendations but showed the sequence of topics. (See Figure 6.6.)

2. The report was submitted and the proposed outline approved. Some modifications were made prior to course development.

The Results

The program was well received by management and leads because it met the needs identified. In addition, the examples used were from real life. The course served as a stepping stone for leads aspiring to move up to the supervisory level. Both the company and the drivers benefitted from the program.

CONCLUSION

A training needs assessment is one of the most basic and common forms of assessment used by HRD professionals in the workplace. This chapter described a five-phase approach for doing such an assessment. The key to performing a successful training needs assessment is to follow a few simple guidelines.

First, adapt and modify your strategy based on the situation. Although it is recommended that more than one data-gathering method be used for a needs assessment, the case shows that a program can be successful with interviews only.

Second, to facilitate the data-collection process, consider using existing or "found" data.

Third, limit the size of the group from which information must be obtained. This simplifies the data-analysis phase considerably. If large groups must be used, be sure that you have established a sound data-collection and analysis methodology.

I. Welcome to Coaching

   A. Welcome

   B. Factors affecting how much you are able to coach

   C. Course objectives

   D. *Exercise:* Think about a coach you had in the past

   E. Are you coaching now?

II. The Coach as Trainer

   A. Giving directions

   B. *Exercise:* Benefits and drawbacks of showing and telling versus not showing and telling

   C. *Exercise:* Lessons learned

III. The Coach As Counselor

   A. Introduction

   B. The ABCs of understanding behavior

   C. Listening empathetically

   D. Giving feedback

   E. Performance coaching: A seven-step model

IV. The Coach As Motivator

   A. Leading by example

   B. Getting to know each person

   C. Incentives and rewards

V. Achieving Success

   A. Challenges faced by lead drivers in their roles as coaches

   B. Lessons learned from others

   C. When and where to coach

   D. Handling problem situations

   E. Working with your supervisor

FIGURE 6.6 *Course Outline*

III

Needs-Assessment Toolkit

TOOLKIT FORM 3.1 *Business Issues Worksheet*

To examine an existing performance problem

1. What are the key business issues that must be addressed?

_____

_____

_____

2. How long have the problems existed?

_____

_____

_____

3. What are the consequences of not solving these problems?

_____

_____

_____

4. Which business processes are being affected by the problems?

_____

_____

_____

5. What are the performance improvement goals?

_____

_____

_____

6. What is preventing goals from being achieved?

_____

_____

_____

TOOLKIT FORM 3.1 *Business Issues Worksheet* (continued)

To address a future performance need

1. What are the key business issues that must be addressed?

_____

_____

_____

_____

2. Why must these issues be addressed?

_____

_____

_____

_____

3. Which business processes are currently being affected?

_____

_____

_____

_____

4. What are the performance improvement goals?

_____

_____

_____

_____

5. What is preventing goals from being achieved?

_____

_____

_____

_____

A Practical Guide to Needs Assessment by Kavita Gupta. Copyright © 1999 Jossey-Bass/Pfeiffer.

TOOLKIT FORM 3.2 *Process Map Worksheet*

A process map shows the steps or activities that are being performed in a business process. A process boundary shows where a business process begins and ends. For example, the process boundary for order management begins when a customer-service unit sends a mail order and ends when a product is received by a customer.

Instructions

1. To show information received from a source OUTSIDE a process boundary such as a customer, customer request, or another business unit, use a RECTANGLE.

2. To show any activity that is being carried out WITHIN a process such as completing a form, use a CIRCLE.

3. To show the FLOW between activities (INPUTS and OUTPUTS), use an ARROW.

Tips for Process Mapping

1. Document steps in sequence. Try to restrict your diagram to major steps at first. Do not become bogged down in too much detail.

2. Begin by identifying the first major process activity, such as processing quotes, as shown in the figure. Determine the flow of information to and from this process. Use single-pointed arrows for information that flows in one direction. For information that flows between two units or processes, use two-pointed arrows.

3. Identify the next major process. Document the inputs and outputs to this process.

4. Link all major processes as well as inputs and outputs.

   If you cannot define intermediate steps, make notes. Come back to this step later.

5. When you have finished creating your process map, retrace steps to verify accuracy of information collected.

TOOLKIT FORM 3.2 *Process Map Worksheet*
(continued)

Process: _____

Questions To Ask

1. What is the sequence of activities that must be performed to complete this process?
2. Who performs each activity?
3. How much time does it take to perform each activity or step?
4. What are the external inputs?
5. Where do internal inputs come from?
6. What are the outputs?
7. Where do the outputs go?

Key:

▭ Department or Unit
⬭ Processing Activity
➤ Flow of Information

A Practical Guide to Needs Assessment by Kavita Gupta. Copyright © 1999 Jossey-Bass/Pfeiffer.

TOOLKIT FORM 3.3 *Gap Analysis Worksheet*

Process	Current Performance Indicators	Gap	Effect
————	————	————	————
————	————	————	————
————	————	————	————
————	————	————	————
————	————	————	————
————	————	————	————
————	————	————	————
————	————	————	————
————	————	————	————
————	————	————	————
————	————	————	————
————	————	————	————
————	————	————	————
————	————	————	————
————	————	————	————
————	————	————	————
————	————	————	————
————	————	————	————
————	————	————	————
————	————	————	————
————	————	————	————
————	————	————	————

TOOLKIT FORM 3.4 *Change Readiness Checklist*

_____ Have clear objectives for the change initiative been established?

_____ Has a leader been assigned to facilitate the change effort?

_____ Does the leader have the requisite interpersonal and organization development skills to facilitate the change initiative?

_____ Are adequate internal resources available for implementing the performance improvement plan?

_____ Are external resources required?

_____ Have reasons for change been communicated to top management?

_____ Is top management committed to implementing the performance improvement plan?

_____ Is top management willing to take risks to implement the performance improvement plan?

_____ Have reasons for change been communicated to middle management?

_____ Is middle management committed to implementing the performance improvement plan?

_____ Have reasons for change been communicated to front-line employees?

_____ Are front-line employees committed to implementing the performance improvement plan?

_____ Have milestones for celebrating successes been established?

_____ Have strategies for motivating and reinforcing those involved in the performance improvement initiative been devised?

_____ Has a follow-up plan to monitor the change initiative been developed?

A Practical Guide to Needs Assessment by Kavita Gupta. Copyright © 1999 Jossey-Bass/Pfeiffer.

TOOLKIT FORM 3.5 *Performance Improvement Planner*

Project Identification Number: _____

Project Description: _____

Project Sponsor (Name/Business Unit): _____

Performance Improvement Goal: _____

_____

_____

Critical Success Factors: _____

_____

_____

_____

Obstacles to Success: _____

_____

_____

_____

Prerequisites for Starting the Project: _____

_____

_____

Project Structure: _____

_____

_____

Team Requirements: _____

_____

Resources: _____

_____

Expected Cost: _____

Benefits: _____

_____

_____

_____

TOOLKIT FORM 3.5 *Performance Improvement Planner* (continued)

Timeline

Milestone	Expected Start Date	Expected Completion Date
1. _____ _____ _____		
2. _____ _____ _____		
3. _____ _____ _____		
4. _____ _____ _____		
5. _____ _____ _____		
6. _____ _____ _____		

Completed By: _____   Approved By: _____

Date: _____   Date: _____

TOOLKIT FORM 4.1 *Competency Project Plan Worksheet*
Detailed Schedule of Events

Task	SC	HRM	SM 1	TP	PL	SM 2	C	Completion Date
Subtotal: (Hours)								

Project Members: (Enter names of project members here)

Key: SC = Steering Committee   HRM = Human Resource Manager   SM1 = Sales Manager 1
         TP = Training Professional   PL = Project Liaison   SM2 = Sales Manager 2   C = Client

TOOLKIT FORM 4.2 *Competency Interview Worksheet*

Name of Interviewer: _____   Date: _____

I. About the Interviewee

Name: _____   Position: _____

Unit: _____   Highest Degree: _____

Previous Training Received: _____

_____

_____

II. About the Interviewee's Job

Name of Manager: _____   Number of Subordinates: _____

Previous Jobs (Year, Position, Company, Location):

_____

_____

_____

_____

_____

_____

_____

_____

1. What are the five main responsibilities of your job?

_____

_____

_____

_____

_____

_____

_____

A Practical Guide to Needs Assessment by Kavita Gupta. Copyright © 1999 Jossey-Bass/Pfeiffer.

TOOLKIT FORM 4.2 *Competency Interview Worksheet* (continued)

2. What skills and abilities do you require to accomplish each of the above?

_____

_____

_____

_____

3. What other skills and abilities do you require to make you successful in your job?

_____

_____

_____

_____

_____

III. About the Interviewee's Work Experiences

4. Think about an incident you experienced that resulted in a successful outcome. What was the context? When did it happen? Who was involved?

_____

_____

_____

_____

_____

_____

5. What did you feel or think?

_____

_____

_____

_____

_____

_____

6. What did you say? Why were these actions and words effective?

_____

_____

_____

_____

_____

_____

_____

7. What were the results? What significance does this event have?

_____

_____

_____

_____

_____

_____

_____

8. Think about an incident you experienced that resulted in an *unsuccessful* outcome. What was the context? When did it happen? Who was involved?

_____

_____

_____

_____

_____

_____

_____

_____

9. What did you feel or think?

_____

_____

_____

_____

_____

_____

10. What did you say? Why were these actions and words ineffective?

_____

_____

_____

_____

_____

11. What are some other actions you did not take at the time that could have helped you succeed?

_____

_____

_____

_____

_____

12. What were the results? What significance does this event have?

_____

_____

_____

_____

_____

_____

TOOLKIT FORM 4.3 *Competency Dictionary Worksheet*

1.

Core Clusters	Definitions

2.

Core Clusters	Definitions

3.

Core Clusters	Definitions

TOOLKIT FORM 4.3 *Competency Dictionary Worksheet* (continued)

4.

Core Clusters	Definitions

5.

Core Clusters	Definitions

6.

Core Clusters	Definitions

TOOLKIT FORM 4.4 *Competency Model Worksheet*

	Core Clusters			
Dimensions				
1.				
2.				
3.				
4.				
5.				
6.				

A Practical Guide to Needs Assessment by Kavita Gupta. Copyright © 1999 Jossey-Bass/Pfeiffer.

TOOLKIT FORM 4.5 *Individual Learning Development Plan for* _____ *(Year)*

Employee Name: _____ Position: _____

Business Unit: _____ Manager: _____

Competency To Be Developed	Learning & Development Activities	Internal & External Support & Resources Needed	Success Measures	Completion Date	Review Date

Employee Signature: _____ Date: _____

Manager Signature: _____ Date: _____

157

TOOLKIT FORM 5.1 *Job Analysis Questionnaire*

Purpose: The purpose of this questionnaire is to gather information about your job.

Directions: Answer all the questions. Return the questionnaire to your supervisor

by _____ .

Sample Questions:

1. List all your major responsibilities. Then prioritize each item by assigning a number to it. For example, assign the number "1" to the responsibility you consider the most important.

_____

_____

_____

_____

_____

_____

_____

_____

2. Why are these responsibilities important to your job?

_____

_____

_____

_____

_____

_____

3. What equipment and tools do you use in your job?

_____

_____

_____

_____

_____

_____

A Practical Guide to Needs Assessment by Kavita Gupta. Copyright © 1999 Jossey-Bass/Pfeiffer.

TOOLKIT FORM 5.1 *Job Analysis Questionnaire* (continued)

4. Describe some specific duties or tasks that you perform in your job. Next to each item, state how often you perform this duty or task.

_____

_____

_____

_____

_____

_____

_____

5. What knowledge do you require to perform your job successfully?

_____

_____

_____

_____

_____

6. What qualities are necessary to make you successful in your job?

_____

_____

_____

_____

_____

7. What prior knowledge, skills, or abilities did you bring to your position that helped to make you successful in your job?

_____

_____

_____

_____

TOOLKIT FORM 5.1 *Job Analysis Questionnaire* (continued)

8. List any courses, workshops, or training programs you attended in the past that you feel have helped you succeed in your job.

_____

_____

_____

_____

_____

_____

9. Describe any other contributing factors that you feel have made you successful in your job.

_____

_____

_____

_____

_____

TOOLKIT FORM 5.2 *Job Training Plan I*

Job Title (Professional/Supervisory/Management):
Department:
Location:

Job Responsibility 1: _____

1. Job Task: _____

2. Job Task: _____

3. Job Task: _____

4. Job Task: _____

5. Job Task: _____

Competencies: _____

Training Requirements: _____

Job Responsibility 2: _____

1. Job Task: _____

2. Job Task: _____

3. Job Task: _____

4. Job Task: _____

5. Job Task: _____

Competencies: _____

Training Requirements: _____

Job Responsibility 3: _____

1. Job Task: _____

2. Job Task: _____

3. Job Task: _____

4. Job Task: _____

5. Job Task: _____

Competencies: _____

Training Requirements: _____

TOOLKIT FORM 5.2 *Job Training Plan I* (continued)

Job Title (Professional/Supervisory/Management):
Department:
Location:

Job Responsibility 4: _____

  1. Job Task: _____

  2. Job Task: _____

  3. Job Task: _____

  4. Job Task: _____

Competencies: _____

Training Requirements: _____

Job Responsibility 5: _____

  1. Job Task: _____

  2. Job Task: _____

  3. Job Task: _____

  4. Job Task: _____

  5. Job Task: _____

Competencies: _____

Training Requirements: _____

Job Responsibility 6: _____

  1. Job Task: _____

  2. Job Task: _____

  3. Job Task: _____

  4. Job Task: _____

  5. Job Task: _____

Competencies: _____

Training Requirements: _____

TOOLKIT FORM 5.3 *Job Training Plan II*

Job Title (Administrative):
Department:
Location:

Job Responsibility 1: _____

  1. Job Task: _____

  2. Job Task: _____

  3. Job Task: _____

  4. Job Task: _____

Knowledge: _____

Skills/Abilities: _____

Standards: _____

Training: _____

Job Responsibility 2: _____

  1. Job Task: _____

  2. Job Task: _____

  3. Job Task: _____

  4. Job Task: _____

Knowledge: _____

Skills/Abilities: _____

Standards: _____

Training: _____

Job Responsibility 3: _____

  1. Job Task: _____

  2. Job Task: _____

  3. Job Task: _____

  4. Job Task: _____

Knowledge: _____

Skills/Abilities: _____

Standards: _____

Training: _____

TOOLKIT FORM 5.3 *Job Training Plan II* (continued)

Job Title (Administrative):
Department:
Location:

Job Responsibility 4: _____

  1. Job Task: _____

  2. Job Task: _____

  3. Job Task: _____

  4. Job Task: _____

Knowledge: _____

Skills/Abilities: _____

Standards: _____

Training: _____

Job Responsibility 5: _____

  1. Job Task: _____

  2. Job Task: _____

  3. Job Task: _____

  4. Job Task: _____

Knowledge: _____

Skills/Abilities: _____

Standards: _____

Training: _____

Job Responsibility 6: _____

  1. Job Task: _____

  2. Job Task: _____

  3. Job Task: _____

  4. Job Task: _____

Knowledge: _____

Skills/Abilities: _____

Standards: _____

Training: _____

TOOLKIT FORM 5.4 *Job Task Analysis Checklist*

_____ Assemble project team.

_____ Select above-average high performers and/or subject-matter experts who will provide input for the work session.

_____ Notify employees' supervisors.

_____ Conduct briefing if necessary.

_____ Prepare job analysis questionnaire.

_____ Distribute or mail questionnaires.

_____ Summarize questionnaires.

_____ Prepare flip chart for session. List key job responsibilities supplied by all participants.

_____ Prepare agenda for work sessions.

_____ Obtain materials for session.

_____ Prepare meeting room for session.

_____ During session refine list of job responsibilities.

_____ Create task statements for each job responsibility.

_____ Omit nonessential tasks.

_____ Identify knowledge, skills, and abilities required to perform tasks.

_____ Identify training requirements to perform job tasks.

_____ Prioritize training needs.

_____ Prepare draft of job training plan.

_____ Submit draft of job training plan to supervisors for approval.

_____ Prepare final draft of job training plan.

_____ Distribute copies of final job training plan.

TOOLKIT FORM 6.1 *Training Needs Assessment Interview Guide*

Name: _____   Date: _____

Interviewer: _____   Interviewee: _____

General Questions

1. Why do you think training is needed?

_____

_____

_____

_____

2. Describe specific instances of how workplace productivity has been affected by lack of training.

_____

_____

_____

_____

3. Give specific examples of how shortfalls in performance have affected unit goals, overall organizational goals, or customer-satisfaction indices. (Add other indicators that are specific to your organization).

_____

_____

_____

_____

_____

4. What other factors (internal or external) do you think are causing performance problems?

_____

_____

_____

_____

A Practical Guide to Needs Assessment by Kavita Gupta. Copyright © 1999 Jossey-Bass/Pfeiffer.

TOOLKIT FORM 6.1 *Training Needs Assessment Interview Guide* (continued)

Questions for Client Contact

5. What are the goals of the assessment?

_____

_____

_____

6. What resources will be available for conducting the assessment (monetary and nonmonetary)?

_____

_____

_____

7. Whose approval must be obtained in order to proceed with the assessment?

_____

_____

_____

8. Which groups must buy in to the concept?

_____

_____

_____

9. What are the most convenient times for collecting data?

_____

_____

_____

10. What is the projected timeline for implementing the training?

_____

_____

_____

11. List characteristics of the target audience, such as age, educational level, learning styles, attitudes toward learning, and computer literacy:

_____

_____

_____

12. What is the approximate size of the target audience by position, geographic location, and so forth?

_____

_____

_____

13. Has the target audience received prior training in this area? If so, what type of training?

_____

_____

_____

14. What are the prerequisites for the program(s)?

_____

_____

_____

15. Will certification be required?

_____

_____

_____

16. Who are the internal and external customers of the target audience?

_____

_____

_____

TOOLKIT FORM 6.2 *Skills Assessment Survey*

The Human Resource Department is conducting a survey of the job requirements of all [name of job function] at [name of company]. The information that is collected will be used to prepare a training plan for all [name of job function]. Your input is vital for ensuring the success of this initiative.

Instructions: This survey should take approximately fifteen to twenty minutes to complete. For each of the following items, please circle the appropriate rating. For items that are not applicable, circle "N.A." Please be candid in your responses.

Key:

1 = Very Low   2 = Low   3 = Medium   4 = High   5 = Very High   N.A. = Not Applicable

Current Level of Proficiency

[Enter skills here]

Example:

1. Obtain product information from customer   1   2   3   4   5   N.A.

Note: Add a place to enter demographic information.

Interpretation of Scores

All items that receive a rating of "3" or below indicate a need for training. The assumption is that the desired rating is "4" or above.

To ensure accuracy of responses, as there is a possibility that ratings may be inflated, do the following:

- Conduct follow-up interviews with unit managers to corroborate information obtained from surveys.

- Consider sending anonymous surveys. (The major disadvantage of this method is that individualized training needs cannot be identified.)

TOOLKIT FORM 6.3 *Customer-Service Training Needs Assessment*
Questionnaire

The Training Department is conducting a customer-service training needs assessment at [name of company]. The information collected will be used to prepare a training plan for all customer-service personnel. Your input is vital for ensuring the success of this initiative.

Instructions: This questionnaire will take approximately twenty-five minutes to complete. Please be candid when responding to the questions.

1. What are the five main responsibilities of your job? List the approximate percent of time you spend on each job responsibility.

_____

_____

_____

_____

_____

2. What competencies do you require to be successful in your job?

_____

_____

_____

_____

3. What are the critical success factors for effective performance in your job?

_____

_____

_____

_____

4. What are the main barriers to your success?

_____

_____

_____

_____

5. What are the most difficult aspects of your job?

_____

_____

_____

_____

_____

_____

6. What should the training priorities for your job function be?

_____

_____

_____

_____

_____

7. What prior customer-service training have you received? List all training received, including training received in previous jobs.

_____

_____

_____

_____

_____

8. What are your preferred learning styles (self-paced, computer-based, classroom)? Describe any others.

_____

_____

_____

_____

_____

TOOLKIT FORM 6.3 *Customer-Service Training Needs Assessment Questionnaire* (continued)

Note: The following portion of the questionnaire can also be distributed to supervisors and other internal or external customers if the instructions are modified.

9. Please complete the following self-assessment, using the following scale:

1 = Very Poor   2 = Poor   3 = Average   4 = Good   5 = Excellent   N.A. = Not Applicable

	1	2	3	4	5	N.A.
a. Knowledge of customer service standards	1	2	3	4	5	N.A.
b. Knowledge of customer service phone etiquette	1	2	3	4	5	N.A.
c. Knowledge of products	1	2	3	4	5	N.A.
d. Knowledge of product rules and regulations	1	2	3	4	5	N.A.
e. Ability to handle customer service calls	1	2	3	4	5	N.A.
f. Ability to respond promptly to requests	1	2	3	4	5	N.A.
g. Ability to handle customer complaints	1	2	3	4	5	N.A.
h. Ability to solve problems quickly	1	2	3	4	5	N.A.
i. Ability to make decisions quickly	1	2	3	4	5	N.A.
j. Ability to negotiate	1	2	3	4	5	N.A.
k. Ability to listen carefully	1	2	3	4	5	N.A.
l. Ability to manage stress	1	2	3	4	5	N.A.

[Add questions of your own.]

Name: _____   Date: _____

Position/Title: _____   Unit: _____

TOOLKIT FORM 6.4 *Management Training Needs Assessment Questionnaire*

The Training Department is conducting a company-wide management training needs assessment at [name of company]. The information we gather will be used to prepare a training plan for all [name of job function]. Your input is vital for ensuring the success of this initiative.

Instructions: This questionnaire will take approximately twenty-five minutes to complete. Please be candid when responding to the questions.

1. What are the five main responsibilities of your job? List the approximate percent of time you spend on each job responsibility.

   _____

   _____

   _____

   _____

   _____

2. What competencies do you require to be successful in your job?

   _____

   _____

   _____

   _____

   _____

3. What are the critical success factors for your effective performance?

   _____

   _____

   _____

   _____

4. What are the main barriers to your success?

   _____

   _____

   _____

   _____

A Practical Guide to Needs Assessment by Kavita Gupta. Copyright © 1999 Jossey-Bass/Pfeiffer.

5. What are the most difficult aspects of your job?

_____

_____

_____

_____

_____

6. What should the training priorities for your job function be?

_____

_____

_____

_____

_____

7. What prior management training have you received? List all training received, including training received in previous jobs.

_____

_____

_____

_____

8. What are your preferred learning styles (self-paced, computer-based training, classroom)? Describe any others.

_____

_____

_____

_____

Name: _____   Date: _____

Position/Title: _____   Unit: _____

Instructions: This survey will take approximately fifteen minutes to complete. Please rate your [managers/subordinates] on the following items, using the key below. Please be candid when responding. Circle your choices.

Key: 1 = Strongly Disagree   2 = Disagree   3 = Somewhat Agree
        4 = Agree   5 = Strongly Agree   N.A. = Not Applicable

Leadership

1. They are visionaries.   1   2   3   4   5   N.A.

2. They serve as coaches and mentors.   1   2   3   4   5   N.A.

3. They encourage teamwork.   1   2   3   4   5   N.A.

4. They treat me and my co-workers fairly.   1   2   3   4   5   N.A.

5. They treat me and my co-workers with respect.   1   2   3   4   5   N.A.

6. They project a positive view of the organization to clients and customers.   1   2   3   4   5   N.A.

Communication

7. They clearly communicate what is expected of me.   1   2   3   4   5   N.A.

8. They clearly communicate what is expected of my co-workers.   1   2   3   4   5   N.A.

9. They keep me informed about critical business issues that may have an impact on my job.   1   2   3   4   5   N.A.

10. They keep me updated about the unit's accomplishments through memos and other communication channels.   1   2   3   4   5   N.A.

11. They are effective in making presentations to others.   1   2   3   4   5   N.A.

12. They establish clear channels of communication between group members.   1   2   3   4   5   N.A.

13. They establish clear channels of communication between this unit and other units.   1   2   3   4   5   N.A.

Performance Management

14. They are genuinely concerned about my job performance.   1   2   3   4   5   N.A.

15. They provide me and co-workers with challenging tasks.   1   2   3   4   5   N.A.

   A Practical Guide to Needs Assessment by Kavita Gupta. Copyright © 1999 Jossey-Bass/Pfeiffer.

TOOLKIT FORM 6.4 *Management Training Needs Assessment Questionnaire*
(continued)

Key: 1 = Strongly Disagree   2 = Disagree   3 = Somewhat Agree
4 = Agree   5 = Strongly Agree   N.A. = Not Applicable

16. They provide opportunities for professional growth
and development.   1   2   3   4   5   N.A.

17. They conduct effective performance appraisal
meetings.   1   2   3   4   5   N.A.

18. They resolve conflicts effectively.   1   2   3   4   5   N.A.

19. They provide feedback at the appropriate time.   1   2   3   4   5   N.A.

Project Management

20. They delegate tasks according to the appropriate
skill and experience level of the group members.   1   2   3   4   5   N.A.

21. They forecast the work load of the group effectively.   1   2   3   4   5   N.A.

22. They plan effectively.   1   2   3   4   5   N.A.

23. They take appropriate corrective action when
necessary.   1   2   3   4   5   N.A.

Customer Service

24. They put the customers' needs before the needs of
the organization.   1   2   3   4   5   N.A.

25. They are sensitive to the needs of customers.   1   2   3   4   5   N.A.

26. They are continually seeking ways to provide
superior service to customers.   1   2   3   4   5   N.A.

27. They are aware of industry standards for customer
service.   1   2   3   4   5   N.A.

Sales

28. They demonstrate effective negotiation skills.   1   2   3   4   5   N.A.

29. They proactively identify sales opportunities with
internal and external customers.   1   2   3   4   5   N.A.

30. They forge strong relationships with internal and
external customers.   1   2   3   4   5   N.A.

TOOLKIT FORM 6.5 *Training Needs Assessment Curriculum Plan I*

	Core Curriculum		
	Year 1	**Year 2**	**Year 3**
Sales Executive			
Sales Manager			
Sales Associate			

TOOLKIT FORM 6.5 *Training Needs Assessment Curriculum Plan I* (continued)

	Advanced Curriculum		
	Year 1	Year 2	Year 3
Sales Executive			
Sales Manager			
Sales Associate			

TOOLKIT FORM 6.6 *Training Needs Assessment Curriculum Plan II*

Year _____

Core Curriculum	Topic	Delivery Medium
Sales Executive		
Sales Manager		
Sales Associate		

Key Workshop = WS   Interactive Video = IV   Video = V
        Workbook = WB   Audio = A   Other = O

  A Practical Guide to Needs Assessment by Kavita Gupta. Copyright © 1999 Jossey-Bass/Pfeiffer.

TOOLKIT FORM 6.6 *Training Needs Assessment Curriculum Plan II* (continued)

Year _____

Advanced Curriculum	Topic	Delivery Medium
Sales Executive		
Sales Manager		
Sales Associate		

Key Workshop = WS   Interactive Video = IV   Video = V
Workbook = WB   Audio = A   Other = O

TOOLKIT FORM 6.7 *Training Needs Assessment Checklist*

The following checklist may be used for a variety of situations: To implement a new system or new technology, to revise or update existing training program(s), or to develop new training program(s). However, because the assessment requirements for each situation differ, use the items that are most applicable to your organization's needs.

Phase I. Gather Preliminary Data

_____ **1.** Have you scheduled preliminary meetings to gather information from your client contact and other key people?

_____ **2.** Have you obtained a senior manager's perspectives about the goals of the assessment?

_____ **3.** Is there consensus about the goals of the needs assessment among those involved?

_____ **4.** Have you identified the educational level of the target audience?

_____ **5.** Have you determined learners' preferred learning styles?

_____ **6.** Have you identified learners' attitudes toward a new system or technology?

_____ **7.** Have you identified computer literacy levels of the target audience?

_____ **8.** Have you identified the prerequisites for using a system or technology?

_____ **9.** Have you identified the prerequisites for revising or updating an existing program?

_____ **10.** Have you identified the prerequisites for developing a new program?

_____ **11.** Have you identified end user requirements for a new system or technology?

_____ **12.** Have you determined what testing or evaluation strategies will be used to measure success?

_____ **13.** Have you determined whether certification will be required?

_____ **14.** Have you identified resources that are available to conduct and implement the assessment?

A Practical Guide to Needs Assessment by Kavita Gupta. Copyright © 1999 Jossey-Bass/Pfeiffer.

———— **15.** Do you require the assistance of external sources, such as subject-matter experts or consultants?

———— **16.** Have you reviewed records, reports, and other pertinent extant data?

———— **17.** Have you obtained input from all other pertinent sources, such as units, archives, internal or external sources?

———— **18.** Have you benchmarked with other existing programs?

Phase II. Plan

———— **19.** Have you established a project plan?

———— **20.** Have you determined what types of data must be collected?

———— **21.** Have you identified sources of data?

———— **22.** Have you determined which data-gathering methods will be most effective?

———— **23.** Have you established a mechanism for tabulating and analyzing results?

———— **24.** Have you notified the appropriate people about the assessment?

———— **25.** Have you obtained approval to proceed with the assessment?

Phase III. Perform Training Requirements Analysis

———— **26.** Have you developed needs assessment tools?

———— **27.** Have you pilot tested needs assessment tools?

———— **28.** Have you determined current knowledge and skill levels?

———— **29.** Have you determined what desired knowledge and skill levels are?

———— **30.** Have you examined what existing training materials, if any, can be used?

———— **31.** Have you identified what non-training interventions, such as job aids, can be used?

———— **32.** Have you identified what factors are impeding learning?

——————— **33.** Have you taken customer needs into account?

——————— **34.** Have you taken the future needs of learners into account?

——————— **35.** Have you determined what the best medium of delivery will be?

——————— **36.** Have you decided whether existing training delivery systems can be used?

——————— **37.** Do current training delivery systems require updating?

——————— **38.** Does the current vendor base require changes?

——————— **39.** Have you determined whether training services must be outsourced?

——————— **40.** Have you identified changes that must be made to the training evaluation system?

——————— **41.** Have you determined what new technological equipment will have to be added?

——————— **42.** Have you determined what additional equipment and resources will have to be obtained?

——————— **43.** Have you determined whether additional personnel will need to be hired and in what positions?

——————— **44.** Have you determined whether and what facility changes must be made?

——————— **45.** Have you established what resources will be needed to implement training?

——————— **46.** Have you determined how supervisors or managers will support learning?

——————— **47.** Have you determined how the current environment will support learning?

Phase IV. Analyze Data

——————— **48.** Have you compiled results?

——————— **49.** Have you identified patterns or deviations in data?

——————— **50.** Have you briefed your client contact and/or senior management about the results of the assessment?

TOOLKIT FORM 6.7 *Training Needs Assessment Checklist* (continued)

Phase V. Prepare Report

———— **51.** Have you established priorities for implementing interventions?

———— **52.** Have you estimated projected costs for implementing each intervention?

———— **53.** Does the report contain all the relevant information?

———— **54.** Is the report precise and concise?

———— **55.** Have you included all the appropriate supporting documents in the appendix?

Glossary

Actuals Current performance or knowledge (Rossett, 1987).

Behavior Actions of a person (Harless, 1970).

Business Goal A statement describing a measure or target that will be achieved during a certain period.

Business Process A group of activities that provide products, deliver services, or manage resources.

Business Unit A department or function within an organization.

Closed-Ended Question A question containing specific options that a respondent must choose from, such as a multiple-choice question.

Competencies Knowledge, skills, attitudes, values, motivations, and beliefs people need in order to be successful in a job.

Competency Dictionary Definition of individual competencies.

Competency Model A composite picture of the competencies necessary for people to be successful in a job function(s).

Core Cluster Competencies grouped together under a broad dimension.

Cost/Benefit Analysis Ratio of the cost of training versus the cost of not training.

Critical Incident	Process of collecting information about important (critical) performance in special situations (incidents) (Rothwell, 1992).
Curriculum	An overall plan containing the objectives, course modules, content outline, and delivery strategies for training people.
Deficiency	How a situation deviates from the ideal (Harless, 1970).
Environment	Conditions surrounding performance, such as the work environment, equipment, tools, or machinery used in performing tasks (Harless, 1970).
Extant Data	A term given to quantitative and qualitative information gathered during the course of a needs assessment.
Focus Group	A data-collection method in which opinions of five to twelve people who share similar expertise (such as operations staff) are sought.
Gap	Difference between what is and what should be, between an actual state (what results are) and a desired state (what results should be) (Kaufman, Rojas, & Mayer, 1993).
Individual Learning Development Plan	An individual plan that shows the development plan, learning activities, support and resources, success indicators, and measures for improving performance.
Job Responsibility	Describes the scope of activities for a job function or job position, such as operations manager.
Job Task	Describes what must be done in order to fulfill a responsibility—usually four to six tasks for each responsibility.

Knowledge	What people must know, such as subject matter, concepts, or facts, in order to do a job.
Learning Channel	A way of acquiring knowledge, skills, and abilities.
Likert Scale	A scale on which respondents are asked to rank or rate values or attitudes.
Mission	A broad statement describing an organization's future plans and directions.
Needs Assessment	Process for pinpointing reasons for gaps in performance or a method for identifying new and future performance needs.
Nominal Scale	A closed-ended question that contains choices not arranged in any prescribed order.
Open-Ended Question	A question that a respondent answers in his or her own words.
Optimals	Desired knowledge or performance (Rossett, 1987).
Performance Improvement Planner	A blueprint that documents all the performance improvement projects that must be undertaken to improve the overall effectiveness of an organization.
Pilot Test	A trial run in which an object, such as a data-collection instrument, is tested for problems or "bugs."
Position Training Plan	A matrix of the knowledge, skills, and abilities needed for an individual to perform a job.
Process Map	A graphical illustration of the steps or activities that are performed in a business.
Process Boundary	An arbitrary "line" that shows where a business process begins and ends.

Qualitative Data	Soft data, such as perceptions, values, attitudes, opinions, or ideas.
Quantitative Data	Hard data, such as indices, sales averages, or number of word processing programs used.
Skills or Abilities	What people must do in order to perform a job.
Standard	A criterion that specifies how a task should be performed.

References

Boyatzis, R. (1982). *The competent manager.* New York: John Wiley.

Brinkerhoff, R., & Gill, S. (1994). *The learning alliance.* San Francisco, CA: Jossey-Bass.

Butruille, S. (1989, March). Be a better job analyst. *Infoline* 8903. Alexandria, VA: American Society for Training and Development.

Callahan, M. (1985, March). Be a better task analyst. *Infoline* 8503. Alexandria, VA: American Society for Training and Development.

Callahan, M. (1985, February). Be a better needs analyst. *Infoline* 8502. Alexandria, VA: American Society for Training and Development.

Dixit, A., & Nalebuff, B. (1991). *Thinking strategically.* New York: W. W. Norton.

Dubois, D. (1993). *Competency-based performance improvement.* Amherst, MA: HRD Press.

Flanagan, J. (1954). The critical incident technique. *Psychological Bulletin, 51,* 327–358.

Gephart, M., & Buren, M. (1996). Building synergy: The power of high performance work systems. *Training and Development, 50*(10), 24–25.

Griffiths, B. (1997, February). *Constructing and validating a competency model.* Unpublished manuscript.

Hammer, M., & Champy, J. (1993). *Reengineering the corporation.* New York: HarperCollins.

Harless, J. (1970). *An ounce of analysis (is worth a pound of objectives)*. Newnan, GA: Harless Performance Guild.

Kaufman, R. (1996). *Strategic thinking*. Alexandria, VA: American Society for Training and Development/Washington, DC: International Society for Performance Improvement.

Kaufman, R., Rojas, A., & Mayer, H. (1993). *Needs assessment: A user's guide*. Englewood Cliffs, NJ: Educational Technology Publications.

Likert, R. (1932). A technique for the measurement of attitudes. *Archives of Psychology, 140*, 1–55.

Mager, R., & Pipe, P. (1997). *Analyzing performance problems* (3rd ed.). Atlanta, GA: Center for Effective Performance.

McLagan, P. (1989). Models for HRD practice. *Training and Development, 43*(9), 50.

McLagan, P. (1980). Competency models. *Training and Development, 34*(12), 23.

Molenda, M., Pershing, P., & Reigeluth, C. (1996). Designing instructional systems. In R. Craig (Ed.), *The ASTD training and development handbook*. New York: McGraw-Hill.

Paul, K., & Bracken, D. (1995). Everything you always wanted to know about employee surveys. *Training and Development, 49*(1), 47.

Phillips, J., & Holton, E.F., III. (Eds.). (1995). *In action: Conducting needs assessment*. Alexandria, VA: American Society for Training and Development.

Porter, M. (1996, November-December). What is strategy? *Harvard Business Review,* p. 62.

Porter, M. (1980). *Competitive strategy*. New York: The Free Press.

Ripley, D. (1997). Joe Harless: An ounce of analysis. In P. Dean & D. Ripley (Eds.), *Performance improvement pathfinders*. Washington, DC: International Society for Performance Improvement.

Robinson, D., & Robinson, J. (1989). *Training for impact*. San Francisco, CA: Jossey-Bass.

Rossett, A. (1987). *Training needs assessment.* Englewood Cliffs, NJ: Educational Technology Publications.

Rothwell, W., & Kazanas, H.C. (1992). *Mastering the instructional design process.* San Francisco, CA: Jossey-Bass.

Rummler, G. (1995). *Improving performance: How to manage the white space in organizations.* San Francisco, CA: Jossey-Bass.

Schwarz, R. (1995). Hiring good facilitators. *Training and Development, 49*(5), 67.

Spencer, L. (1995). The economic value of competencies: Measuring the ROI of your training and development programs. *Proceedings of 2nd International Conference on Using Competency-Based Tools and Applications to Drive Organizational Performance* (p. 364). Lexington, MA: Linkage/Cleveland, OH: Case Western Reserve University.

Additional Resources

CHAPTER ONE

Gilbert, T. (1978). *Human competence: Engineering worthy performance.* New York: McGraw-Hill.

Harless, J. (1970). *An ounce of analysis (is worth a pound of objectives).* Newman, GA: Harless Performance Guild.

Kaufman, R. (1997). Needs assessment basics. In *The guide to performance improvement.* San Francisco, CA: Jossey-Bass/Pfeiffer.

Kaufman, R. (1996). *Strategic thinking.* Alexandria, VA: American Society for Training and Development/Washington, DC: International Society for Performance Improvement.

Kaufman, R. (1994). A needs assessment audit. *Performance and Instruction, 33*(2), 107–109.

Mager, R., & Pipe, P. (1997). *Analyzing performance problems* (3rd ed.). Atlanta, GA: Center for Effective Performance.

McLagan, P. (1996). Creating the future of HRD. *Training and Development, 50*(1), 60–65.

McLagan, P. (1989). Models for HRD practice. *Training and Development, 43*(9), 50.

Rossett, A. (1987). *Training needs assessment.* Englewood Cliffs, NJ: Educational Technology Publications.

Rummler, G. (1996). In search of the holy performance grail. *Training and Development, 50*(4), 26–32.

Rummler, G. (1995). *Improving performance: How to manage the white space in organizations.* San Francisco, CA: Jossey-Bass.

Westgaard, O. (1997). Describing a performance improvement specialist. *Performance Improvement, 36*(6), 10–15.

CHAPTER TWO

Oppenheim, A. (1993). *Questionnaire design.* New York: Books International.

Phillips, J., & Holton, E. F., III. (Eds.). (1995). *In action: Conducting needs assessment.* Alexandria, VA: American Society for Training and Development.

CHAPTER THREE

Brinkerhoff, R., & Gill, S. (1994). *The learning alliance.* San Francisco, CA: Jossey-Bass.

Goffee, R., & Jones, G. (1996, November/December). What holds the modern company together? *Harvard Business Review,* pp. 146–148.

Kaufman, R. (1997). A strategic planning framework: Mega planning. In *The guidebook for performance improvement.* San Francisco, CA: Jossey-Bass/Pfeiffer.

Larkin, T., & Larkin, S. (1996, May/June). Reaching and changing front-line employees. *Harvard Business Review,* pp. 95–104.

Porter, M. (1980). *Competitive strategy.* New York: The Free Press.

Rummler, G. (1995). *Improving performance: How to manage the white space.* San Francisco, CA: Jossey-Bass.

Rummler, G. (1997). Managing an organization as a system. *Training, 34*(2), 68–74.

Wheatley, M. (1996). *A simpler way.* San Francisco, CA: Berrett-Koehler.

CHAPTER FOUR

Boyatzis, R. (1980). *The competent manager.* New York: John Wiley.

McLagan, P. (1996). Creating the future of HRD. *Training and Development, 50*(1), 60–65.

Spencer, L. (1993). *Competence at work.* New York: John Wiley.

CHAPTER FIVE

Carlisle, K. (1986). *Analyzing jobs and tasks.* Englewood Cliffs, NJ: Educational Technology Publications.

Mueller, N. (1997, November/December). Using SMEs to design training. *Technical Training, 8*(8), 14–19.

Phillips, J., & Holton, E. F., III. (Eds.). (1995). *In action: Conducting needs assessment.* Alexandria, VA: American Society for Training and Development.

CHAPTER SIX

Brethower, D. (1997, November/December). Rapid analysis: Matching solutions to changing situations. *Performance Improvement, 36*(10), 16–21.

Darraugh, B., & Sharpe, C. (1997). How to conduct a cost-benefit analysis. *Infoline,* 9007. Alexandria, VA: American Society for Training and Development.

Fulop, M., Loop-Bartick, K., & Rossett, A. (1997, July). Using the world wide web to conduct a needs assessment. *Performance Improvement, 36*(6), 22–27.

Gupta, K. (1998). The mini problem-indicator inventory. In *The 1998 annual: Volume 1, training.* San Francisco, CA: Jossey-Bass/Pfeiffer.

Gupta, K. (1996, November/December). Conducting a mini needs assessment. *Infoline,* 9611. Alexandria, VA: American Society for Training and Development.

Hamilton, M., & Hamilton, S. (1997). Turbo OJT can redefine workplace learning. *Technical Training, 8*(8), 8–12.

Kaufman, R. (1997). Needs assessment basics. In *The guidebook for performance improvement.* San Francisco, CA: Jossey-Bass/Pfeiffer.

Mager, R., & Pipe, P. (1997). *Analyzing performance problems* (3rd ed.). Atlanta, GA: Center for Effective Performance.

Robinson, D., & Robinson, J. (1995). *Performance consulting.* San Francisco, CA: Berrett-Koehler.

Rossett, A. (1987). *Training needs assessment.* Englewood Cliffs, NJ: Educational Technology Publications.

Yaney, J. (1997, September). Questionnaires help in problem-analysis. *Performance Improvement, 36*(8), 28–33.

Zemke, R. (1998, March). How to do a needs assessment when you don't have time. *Training, 35*(3), 38–44.

Index

About the Author

KAVITA GUPTA has developed training programs for corporations and conducted workshops for several universities in New England. She has been an active member of the American Society for Training and Development and has served on several boards. Ms. Gupta has also published several articles. She holds a master's degree in instructional systems technology from Indiana University.

Toolkit Forms on Disk

THE MINIMUM CONFIGURATION needed to utilize the files included on this disk is a computer system with one 3.5" floppy disk drive capable of reading double-sided high-density IBM formatted floppy disks and word processing or desktop publishing software able to read Microsoft WORD 6.0/95 files. Document memory needs will vary, but your system should be capable of opening file sizes of 50+K. No monitor requirements other than the ones established by your document software need be met.

Each of the Toolkit forms in your book has been saved onto the enclosed disk as a Microsoft WORD 6.0/95 file. These files can be opened with many Windows- and Macintosh-based word processors or desktop publishers for viewing or editing as you see fit. The files were originally created and saved as a WORD 6.0/95 DOC file by Microsoft Word 97. Not all software will read the files exactly the same, but the DOC format is an honest attempt by Jossey-Bass/Pfeiffer Publishers to preserve the composition of the figures such as borders, fonts, character attributes, bullets, etc., as accurately as possible.

Copy all DOC files to a directory/folder in your computer system. To read the files using your Windows-based document software, select *File* from the main menu followed by *Open* to display the Open dialog box. Set the correct drive letter and subdirectory shown in the Open dialog box by using the *Look in* control. In the Files of type text box enter *.doc to display the list of DOC files available in the subdirectory.

Each file name is coded to its Toolkit form in the text to make it easy for you to find the one you want. For example, Toolkit Form 3.1 has been named TK03-01.DOC. You can open the file by either double-clicking your mouse on the file name that you want to open or by clicking once on the file name to select it and then once on the *Open* command button.